CONTENTS

GW01458238

TIME LINE IN CORNWALL

Note: all dates in this Guide are expressed as BCE (Before Common Era) = BC and CE (Common Era) = AD. Dates given in the following timeline are approximate.

Paleolithic: 70,000 - 8000 BCE [No evidence for occupation in Cornwall]

Mesolithic: 8000 - 4500 BCE - Britain separates from Continent. Hunter-gatherers make seasonal visits to Cornwall. Microliths (flint flakes) found at a few sites.

Neolithic: 4500 - 2000 BCE - First settlements - beginning of farming. Tor enclosures, cromlechs, & long barrows begin to be built - entrance graves later.

Bronze Age: 2500 - 600 BCE - People lived in Round Houses & domesticated animals. Stone circles, standing stones, stone rows & round barrows constructed.

Iron Age: 800 BCE - 500 CE - Round houses continued, but later on Courtyard Houses become fashionable, with fogous. Hill forts, cliff castles & rounds also constructed.

Romano-Cornish: 500 - 800 CE - Some evidence for Roman occupation in Cornwall but much less than in England. Forts & houses, but no villas.

This booklet covers nearly all the sites in West Penwith from these prehistoric periods, but does not include sites from later, such as Early Christian Crosses and Inscribed Stones.

Front cover photograph: The Nine Maidens stone circle at Boskednan. All photographs & maps © Cheryl Straffon. Thanks to Andy Norfolk for artwork on front & back covers and pages 2, 3, 11, 20, 22, 39 & 49, and to Craig Weatherhill for plans and drawings on pages 4, 6, 8, 9, 35, 40, 41, 42 & 43.

INTRODUCTION

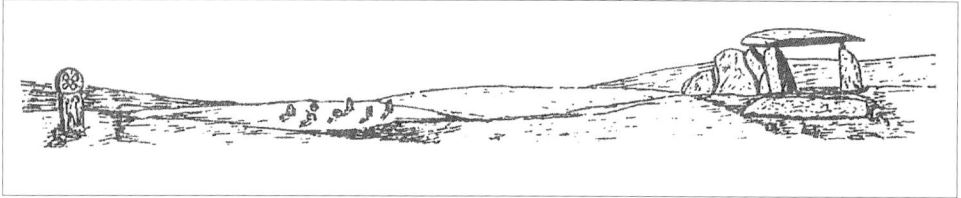

It was 19 years ago that the first edition of "The Earth Mysteries Guide to Ancient Sites in West Penwith" was first published, the first of what turned out to be 4 such Guides covering all of Cornwall and the Isles of Scilly. In the intervening years, other books have been published about the ancient sites, but this Guide remains still the only such booklet that gives full details of the sites and all the 'Earth Mysteries' information known about them. Now, with this first major revision of the Guide, with full colour photographs of the sites, it should serve a new generation for many years to come.

Earth Mysteries is an umbrella term, that covers 'alternative archaeological' research into the meaning and purpose of the sites built by ancient peoples, and can include the location and alignment of sites in the landscape, their anomalous magnetic and radioactive qualities, their astronomical orientations, the folklore linked to them, and the psychic and spiritual phenomena experienced at them. The first Edition of this booklet included much of this information, but in the 19 years since then, much more has been discovered and reported in the pages of *Meyn Mamvro* magazine. This new Revision includes updates of that research, and brings together as much useful information on the sites as can be crammed into 52 pages!

The sites are divided into 8 main sections: each section starts with an introduction to give a flavour of the special qualities of the particular type of site. This is followed by a comprehensive guide to the sites themselves, which includes information not only on the main ones but also the more obscure and little known ones for those who would like to investigate further. There are location maps to give a pattern of distribution, and also 8 figure National Grid references to precisely fix the sites (all should be prefixed by SW). The OS Explorer map no.102 at a scale of 1:25000 remains the best aid to finding the sites.

The recent decades have seen a much improved system of caring for and looking after the sites. In particular, CASPN (Cornish Ancient Sites Protection Network) has been instrumental in setting up a system of Site Monitors, and oversees a reporting system for damage and vandalism, and a monthly Clear-up scheme at various sites. More details can be found on their website www.cornishancientsites.com. If you would like to support their work, please consider joining FOCAS (Friends of Cornwall's Ancient Sites). A form can be found on the website, or write to 24 Queen Street, St.Just, Penzance TR19 7JW, or telephone 01736-793905. Site damage can be reported to 01736-787186 or 01736-787522.

stone circles

The stone circles of West Penwith - mysterious places of the earth. Perhaps temples of the people where sacred rites were performed by the light of the moon. Perhaps here at times of magic, the megalithic community celebrated the creative power of the Goddess, in festivals when "the energy-tides of the unseen flowed strongly around and through the earth". Were the earth channels then wide open to receive her spirit: a spirit used for healing and fertility by the people? And did those people dance nine times around the stones, "waking the earth from her dreams below"? Nine times, nine moons, the nine maidens. At Boskednan, Boscawen-ûn, the Merry Maidens and Tregeseal, young girls were turned to stone, perhaps Priestesses from the mists of time. We touch the stones and wonder if we are touching their spirits. The stones still live - we feel their warmth, sense their energies, watch them change with the seasons and the passage of the days. We see them in the first rays of dawn, dancing ourselves and them alive at Boskednan on the summer solstice. We see them in the bright light of day, resting our backs on the centre stone of Boscawen-ûn, singing and sharing friendship. We see them in the setting rays of the sun, its light casting long fingers of stone across the circle at the Merry Maidens, shadow paths of the Celtic twilight. And we see them at night under the full moon at Tregeseal, white and cold, and we give them our offerings of flowers or corn or love.

They are ever changing and yet ever constant. Approach them with respect, treat them with care, for they have been there for many thousands of years and they are infinitely old and wise. Study their alignments, dowse their energies, follow their leys, explore and touch their individual stones. But leave them as you find them - in a field, on the moors, in a hollow. For they are there when you are gone, and in their subtle ways they never reveal all of their secrets to you. Love and respect them for this, and remember that, like the moon, you can know them intimately and yet never know them at all. In West Penwith they wait for you, these sacred rings of stone. In them you will find yourself.

MERRY MAIDENS [4327 2451]

The most accessible and well-known of sites, lying beside the B3315 Penzance-Lamorna road. It is also one of the best-preserved in Britain, its 19 stones being still in situ with only 3 having to be re-erected in the late 19th century. The stones are equally spaced with an entrance gap on the north-eastern side, and vary in height between 0.9m & 1.4m (3-4½ ft) tall, with the tallest ones to the SW and the shortest to the NE. There are also two sets of 2 stones buried in the ground to the south-east of the circle, one of which is still quite prominent, which may have formed part of a processional way to the site. The circle is on a sloping field with the twin hills of Chapel Carn Brea and Bartinney visible to the west, and several fields away to the north-east the **Pipers** standing stones are probable outliers to the circle *[see page 12]*. There was also formerly a possible second circle in the field to the west of the main circle, known as the Boleigh circle [4314 2444].

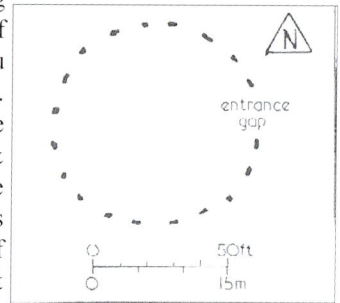

Another outlier is visible in a field hedge to the south of west of the circle. This is the **Gûn Rith** standing stone *[see page 12]*. An **alignment** runs from this menhir through the circle and its gap (following the public footpath), on to a stone in a hedge [4343 2452], touches the site of a destroyed stone circle (Tregurnow) at 4375 2455, and finishes at Borah, a farmhouse whose Cornish name means "the place of the witch" (Bos-wra). There may be a memory here of a 'via sacra' or sacred way walked by ancient peoples as part of a ceremony in the land. This notion is strengthened by the observation of Sir Norman Lockyer, the Astronomer Royal at the beginning of the 20th century, who said that the appearance of the Pleiades star system above the circle at the end of April in 1960 BCE would have warned of the rising sun for the festival of Beltane. The site is Bronze Age (2500-2000 BCE), a date that was presaged by the antiquarian T.C.Lethbridge who in the 1960s used a dowsing pendulum to give a date of 2540 BCE.

The circle has been checked on at least 4 separate occasions for anomalous **radiation** counts. Alan Bleakley in 1982 found higher than average reading inside the circle, but subsequent visits found the reverse. In 1985 Don Robins found that geiger readings halved when he moved inside the circle, and these lower readings were subsequently confirmed by Meyn Mamvro geiger monitoring sessions in 1987 & 1988. Other stone circles have produced similar results, and it does seem that there is an unexplained phenomenum of a radiation 'sanctuary' in the middle of some circles at some times. Whether the people who built the circle were aware of this is part of the mystery.

There is some anecdotal evidence of **electro-magnetic** energy being discharged from the stones in the form of 'tingling' or low-grade electric shocks. Hamish Miller recorded this in 1988, and when he later rigorously dowsed the circle he found spiral **energy** patterns coming from each of the stones and lines of energy flowing out of the site *[diagram right]*. On another occasion CEMG (Cornish Earth Mysteries Group) dowsed the site, and by following one of the energy lines found a 'marker' stone in a nearby hedge at 4322 2483.

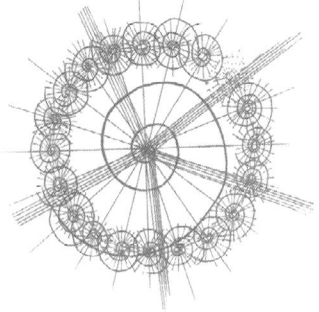

The **magnetic field** was also measured at all the stones, at the centre of the circle and at four points outside. Results at the stones varied between 25-28 µt to 45 µt against the normal British field strength of 47 µt, but the low figures may be the result of sampling error. No significant **ultrasound** noises have been picked up.

Some strange **light and sound** phenomena have been recorded at this site. Rodney Blunsdon and a friend were at the circle with cameras at midnight on a clear night. They had three cameras between them, but inside the circle no flashes on any of the cameras would work. However when the films were developed there were pictures of Rod illuminated with a brilliant white light. The photo also showed anomalous BOLs (balls of light) floating around in front of the stones. At the time, they also heard strange voices, speaking words in a language not understood, together with humming and singing, though there was no-one else present.

Five **leys** (straight lines linking ancient sites in the landscape) have been noted crossing the circle:
[1] The line from Gûn Rith hedge stone through the circle to a stone in a hedge [4343 2452], to the site of the destroyed Tregurnow circle [4375 2455], to Borah Farmhouse.
[2] Boscawen-Ros east menhir [4281 2394] through the circle to the NE Piper [4355 2482], to the Sheffield menhir [4585 2752].
[3] Boscawen-Ros west menhir [4277 2393] to a tumulus [4308 2428], through the circle to a destroyed tumulus [4334 2459] to the SW Piper [4348 2475].
[4] From the circle to the destroyed Boleigh circle [4314 2444], to a destroyed tumulus [4292 2435], which may have denoted the Imbolc and Samhain sunset in Feb & Nov.
[5] From the circle to Tregiffian Barrow [4304 2442] to Boskenna Cross [4258 2426], to Boskenna Gate Cross [4204] 2407, which may have denoted the Beltane (May) sunrise.

BOSCAWEN-ÛN [4122 2736]

This circle is in a very evocative place, being placed in an enclosure hidden amongst fields in the centre of the Penwith peninsula. Two pathways to it are possible, one leading off the A30 through fields, where it appears like a distant vision (with a great view over the site from the rocky outcrop called Creeg Tol on the right hand side of the path); and the other through a sunken lane from Boscawen-ûn farmyard.

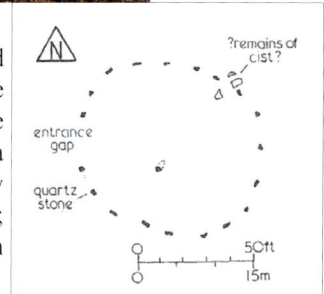

The circle was mentioned in the medieval Welsh Triads, where it was given as one of the three principal gorsedds (Druidic meeting-places) in Britain, and in 1928 the revived Gorsedd of the Bards of Cornwall was inaugerated here. It is a fine circle (or to be more accurate, ellipse) consisting of 19 stones (restored), ranging in height from 0.9m (3ft) to 1.4m (4½ft) with an entrance gap to the west. One of the stones on the south-western side is uniquely made of quartz *[photo right]*, although Duloe circle near Looe in east Cornwall has 8 stones of quartz, and there were 5 quartz menhirs on St. Breock Downs near St. Columb Major. Quartz was evidently a sacred stone for ancient peoples, which may have something to do with the piezo-electric charge generated by the quartz crystal; or may be, as the archaeologist Aubrey Burl suggested, because the gleaming white quarz was seen as a reflection or aspect of the Moon Goddess. One of the few stone circles to be excavated in Cornwall, the Hurlers central on Bodmin Moor, was found to have been built on a bed of small quartz crystals, and dowsers have suggested that the same applies to other stone circles.

There was formerly a stone circle about 1mile to the SW at Higher Trevorian [4169 2625].

There is also an off-centre leaning stone 2.4m (8ft) high, but it is not known whether this stone was always leaning at this angle or whether it has slipped over the years. It has been at an angle since at least 1796 when Borlase drew it. It points in the direction of the midsummer sunrise, whose first rays illuminate the bottom of the stone and two possible axe heads carved on it *[photo right]*. Axes were important to the Neolithic and Bronze-Age peoples as ritual objects, and Cornish greenstone axes were traded with other tribes in England and elsewhere, so this carving on the centre stone is probably a sacred symbol. There is also another possible **alignment** within the circle. An observer standing on the opposite side of the circle from the centre and quartz stones would see the sun set directly between the two stones at Imbolc and Samhain (early Feb & Nov).

The circle was checked for **radiation** in 1992 by CEMG. The outer stones had high counts (average 18 cpm) compared to a background of 12 cpm. The centre of the circle was lower (12 cpm) but the real surprise was the quartz stone that had much lower readings than the other 18 stones and the centre stone. The circle has also been checked for **ultrasound & compass deflections:** no significant variations were found, but a surveyor for South West Water remarked that he experienced total compass disorientation at the site. It has been extensively dowsed for **energy lines** and many have been found running through and around the circle. Hamish Miller found a strong line (the Mary line) entering the circle at an angle of 13° east of north, and then turning at the base of the centre stone and veering off at an angle of 53° east of north that corresponded with the ridge of the leaning stone. Other lines were also found and Hamish commented that "the impression was of a nerve ganglion ... a nervous system that was alive and functioning irrespective of whether Homo Sapiens comprehended it or not".

Eight **leys** have been noted crossing the circle:
[1] From a missing stone at 4031 2719 to the circle, to a stretch of ancient track, to Trenuggo cross [4281 2764], on to Tresvennack menhir [4418 2788].
[2] From the circle to two (now destroyed) intervisible stones at 4041 2721 & 4031 2719.
[3] From the circle to a fallen stone [4182 2707], Trelew menhir [4217 2693], Toldavas stone [4266 2671], to Castallack stone [4540 2545]. Imbolc/Samhain (Feb/Nov) sunrise?
[4] Menhir in a field near the circle [4149 2762], through the circle to a stone at 3978 2594.
[5] Botrea Barrow [4031 3133] to Courtyard House [4042 3076], Brane cross [4090 2877], Goldherring Courtyard House settlement [4120 2830] to edge of circle, to missing stone [4152 2626], to site of Trevorian cross [4155 2601] to Boskenna Gate cross [4201 2407].
[6] From the circle to Trevorgans menhir [4047 2614] to St.Levan cross [3820 2236].
[7] Destroyed Carn Brea stone [3814 2799] to circle, to Redhouse 1 stone [4480 2663] to the site of a lost stone [c4559 2648] to St.Clements Isle off Mousehole.
[8] From the circle to Newham farm menhir [4172 2916] to Lanyon Quoit [4298 3369] to Nine Maidens circle outlier [4399 3516].

TREGESEAL [3866 3238]

This circle lies to the south of Carn Kenidjack, a strangely-shaped rocky outcrop/tor enclosure on the moors near to St.Just, associated with legends of the dead and supernatural beings, as well as anomalous earth-lights. The circle now has 19 stones standing, though it was much disturbed in the past. Most were re-erected in the 1920s by 'persons unknown' and some in the 1980s. The stones range in height from 0.8m (2½ft) to 1.5m (5ft) and are equally spaced with a gap in the south-western side, but a former quarry encroaches on its western flank.

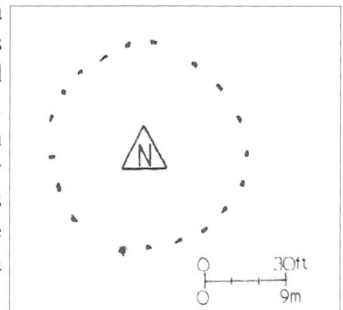

There was formerly a second circle due west of the extant one at 3861 3237 which was destroyed in the 19th & early 20th centuries, although some stones are now incorporated in the Cornish hedge. Also a third circle, again due west at 3857 3257, has been identified from crop marks, but this may have been a cairn circle. There was originally a great concentration of circles, barrows, enclosures and other monuments on Tregeseal Common *[see Meyn Mamvro no.2 p.2-5]*.

The circle has been checked for **radiation** anomalies. No really significant results were found, although the circle stones and a point near the centre were slightly below background. **Water dowsing** revealed that this was the point where six underground streams meet. Four **leys** have been noted crossing the circle:

[1] Tregeseal chambered cairn [3805 3213] through the circle to Boswens menhir [4001 3290] to West Lanyon Quoit [4231 3379] to stone in hedge [4270 3395] to Mulfra Courtyard House settlement [454 349]. This is the direction of the Beltane/May sunrise.
[2] Circle to barrow [3882 3248] to destroyed barrow [3906 3260] to Nine Maidens circle [4343 3512].
[3] Circle to Lanyon Quoit [4298 3369] to Carfury menhir [4400 3400] to Chysauster Courtyard House settlement [472 350]
[4] Circle to Trelew menhir [4217 2693], Caer Bran [408 291], to NE Piper [4354 2482].

NINE MAIDENS (BOSKEDNAN) [4343 3512]

This circle is on open moorland, approachable either from Ding Dong mine or the lane that runs from beside the Mên-an-Tol. It is now somewhat ruined, with only 11 stones standing out of 19 when seen by Borlase in the 19th century. The tallest stone is 2m (6½ft) in height and the rest between 1.0m (3ft) & 1.3m (4ft). Two stones were recently (2005) re-erected, and now the two portal stones frame the view to the rocky outcrop of Carn Gulva on the horizon. There may originally have been a processional way from the circle to this 'holy hilltop', perhaps thought of as the dwelling place of the spirits of the ancestors, or the Gods/Goddesses. There was also formerly a standing stone as outlier to the circle, 43 paces to the NW, which marked the direction of the midsummer solstice sun set, but now only a stump remains. The remains of a barrow intrude on to the edge of the circle, and there are other barrows nearby, one of which stands prominently on the summit of a ridge *[see p.32]*.

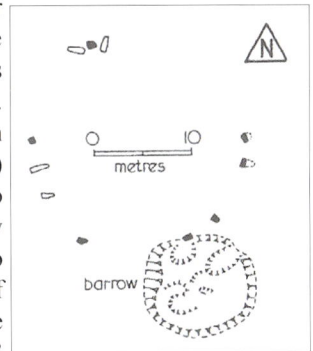

As at Tregeseal, six curving **water lines** have been dowsed to meet at a point just offset from the geometrical centre of the circle. **Radiation** readings taken in 1982 at 4 different sessions consistently produced readings less than half background (12 cpm against 30 cpm). Three **leys** have been noted crossing the circle:

Midsummer solstice sunset from circle over stump of outlier stone

[1] From Tregeseal circle through 2 barrows to this circle *[see Tregeseal 2 alignment]*
[2] Boswens menhir [4001 3298] to circle to line of boundary stones.
[3] Circle to West Lanyon Quoit [4231 3379] to crossroads at 4061 3175, to barrow [4032 3141, to tumulus [3725 2774] to Sennen menhir [3546 2557].

9

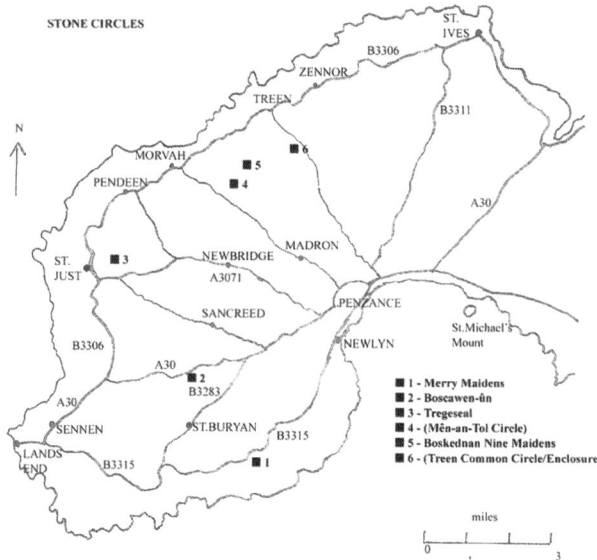

STONE CIRCLES

1 - Merry Maidens
2 - Boscawen-ûn
3 - Tregeseal
4 - (Mên-an-Tol Circle)
5 - Boskednan Nine Maidens
6 - (Treen Common Circle/Enclosure

OTHER SITES

Treen Common (Porthmeor)
[4446 3666]. Borlase noted this as 'Zennor Cirque' - a large ring of 14 erect and fallen stones. It may in fact be part of an Iron Age settlement enclosure. A midsummer sunrise **alignment** to a notch over Zennor Hill has been suggested.

Mên-an-Tol [4264 3493] *See p.20.* This site with its holed stone and uprights has been identified as the remains of a stone circle, consisting of 19 stones, of which traces of 11 are still visible as stumps in ground.

CONCLUSIONS

The places where the circles were built seem to have been chosen for some special qualities. It may be because that is where underground streams met and crossed, and/or where there were low radiation levels or magnetic anomalies, which ancient peoples may have been able to dowse naturally. It may also have been to do with the surrounding landscape. At all 4 main circles, there are distinctive hills and tors: from the Merry Maidens and Creeg Tol above Boscawen-ûn, the twin 'holy hills' of Chapel Carn Brea and Bartinney are distinctive features on the horizon; from Tregeseal the tor enclosure of Carn Kenidjack forms a dominating shape, and may have had a processional way running to it from the circle; and at Boskednan Nine Maidens the tor enclosure of Carn Gulva performed the same function. These tor enclosures had been occupied (if only seasonally) by the Neolithic ancestors of the Bronze Age people who built the circles, so they may have taken on a special resonance or significance in the landscape for them, and may have been thought of as the dwelling places of the spirits of the ancestors or Gods/Goddesses.

The fact that all the stone circles have or had 19 stones is probably not a coincidence. We know from other places (for example, the Aberdeenshire Recumbent Stone Circles) that the megalithic builders deliberately constructed their monuments to frame and view the rising and setting moon at its standstill position, which occurs every 18.6 years. In addition the sun and moon return to their positions relative to each other every 19 years (metonic cycle). In West Cornwall, this may have been symbolically represented by the 19 stones of the circles. Other standing stones would also have been erected at a distance from the circles, making certain alignments to significant solar and astronomical events, which marked the festival/ritual times of the year. The ritual activity at the sites, working in harmony with the natural electromagnetic earth currents, would over a period of time generate strong energy patterns at the sites, the ley lines and energy lines that are dowsable today. The stone circles are the nodal points of this earth energy network.

standing stones

Standing stones - or to give them their Cornish names, menhirs - are dotted over the Penwith landcape like acupuncture needles on the body of the earth. Look over any hedge, or through any farm gate and there you may see one, standing proud and strong, even after 5000 or so years. They have seen many generations come and go, their sacred land has been turned into fields and farms, their use forgotten, and yet they remain, mysterious anachronisms from a time long past. Some are tall and impressive, like the Pipers and Tresvennack pillar, towering over mere mortals as we look up to their top and beyond to the sky; others are smaller but more approachable, like Trevorgans and Porthmeor, inviting us to touch their surfaces and explore their shapes. Others still, like Boswens and the Blind Fiddler, seem to have been deliberately shaped to look different from different sides and viewpoints. Many of them in this small peninsula are visible one from the other, usually as dots on the land at the edges of the horizon.

They seem to call us to follow a trail across the country, a trail that cuts across field boundaries and ignores modern roads and buildings, a trail as old as the stones themselves, a trail we could perhaps call a 'ley-path', a living trail on the sacred earth, perhaps not dissimilar to that followed by the aboriginal Australians as they walk their 'dream-paths', communing with the spirit of the earth. The menhirs are the markstones of these sacred paths, and they seem to grow out of the earth herself, perhaps covered with moss and lichen like Chyenhal, overgrown with ivy and flowers like Castallack Carn, surrounded by daffodils in Spring like Treverven, hidden in the hedge like Chyangwens and Sennen, standing free and high on the moors like Boswens and Watch Croft, or nestling in a sacred grove and covered in bluebells like Carfury. So many stones to visit, each different in their own way, each individual and special. Go and enjoy them, spend some time with them - they will reward the searching a thousandfold.

11

MERRY MAIDENS/LAMORNA AREA

The Pipers [north-east 4354 2482 - *below left;* south-west 4350 2474 - *below right*].

The two tallest menhirs now standing in Cornwall, the NE at 4.6m (15 ft) & the SW in the next field at 4.1m (13½ ft).
Excavated by Borlase in 1871 but no finds. The 2 stones if aligned point to the NW edge of the Merry Maidens circle. Leys:
NE stone [1] Sheffield stone - NE Piper - Merry Maidens - Boscawen-Ros east.
[2] Tumulus 4327 2469 - NE Piper - Castallack Carn stone - Mousehole chapel.
[3] NE Piper - Drift stones - Carfury stone.
[4] NE Piper - Trelew - Tregeseal circle.
[5] Kemyel A & B - NE Piper - Alsia well.
SW stone [1] SW Piper - destroyed tumulus c4334 2459 - Merry Maidens - tumulus 4308 2428 - Boscawen-Ros west.
[2] SW Piper - Kerris - Ennis Farm.
There may originally have been a third Piper, mentioned as a tradition in 1939, but possibly referring to Gûn Rith, or a fallen stone in a hedge at 4360 2490.

Gûn Rith [4294 2448] This 3.2m (10½ ft)

stone stands in a hedge to the SW of the Merry Maidens. Excavated by Borlase in 1871 who found a beach pebble. Fell down and was re-erected in 2003 - some suggestions that it is actually upside down.
Ley to Merry Maidens & beyond *[see p.4]*

Boscawen- Ros [east in field 4281 2394; west in hedge 4278 2393]. These 2 stones

were knocked down in the early 20thC; the eastern one was re-erected in the field. The stump of what may have been a third stone is in a nearby field at 4260 2371. Leys: East stone - See Piper NE [1] ley. West stone [1] See Piper SW ley [2] Newham farm - Trelew - Boscawen-Ros west

Treverven [4082 2399

In a field a mile west of the Merry Maidens & a mile south of St.Buryan is this 2m (7ft) isolated menhir. Ley: Treverven stone - Kerris stone - Faughan hill fort.
Even further west there were formerly 2 stones in a field near Selena Farm [3974 2399]. The remains of one can still be found in the hedge *[see p.14]*.

Castallack [4540 2545]. About a mile to

the east from the Merry Maidens above Lamorna lie a number of stones. This one is notable for cup marks near the base, 7 in one line & 2 below.
Ley: [1] see Boscawen-ûn circle ley [3] [2]Kemyel C stone - Castallack - Kerris

Castallack Carn [4474 2537] is nearby, a 1.8m (6ft) high stone, very overgrown.
Ley: See Piper NE [2].   Formerly other stones at 4550 2513 & 4494 2540.

Swingate stones. On the plateau above Lamorna Cove are several more stones: **Swingate A** [4570 2517] *photo left* is a 2m (6ft) high triangular-shaped stone on a ley to the Castallack stone and the Blind Fiddler stone.

Swingate B [4582 2524] is a 1.5m (4½ft) upright in the next field (lying nearly on the end of Ley [3] from Boscawen-ûn circle - *see p.7*). **Swingate D** [4582 2539] is a smallish triangular stone in the next field, and **Swingate C (Kemyel Drea)** [4616 2522] *photo right* lies southwards, a 2m (6ft) stone pointing towards St. Michael's Mount at a midsummer solstice sunrise angle.

Kemyel stones. Moving southwards towards Lamorna, we come to an area between Kemyel Crease and Kemyel Wartha. Here there are 3 more stones. **Kemyel A** [4569 2467] *photo left* is a 2m (6¼ft) triangular stone, which points at the tip of the Lizard across Mounts Bay at an angle that would indicate a Samhain/Imbolc (Nov & Feb) sunrise. It forms an alignment with a stone in the hedge **Kemyel B** [2573 2466] and runs on to the Pipers NE & Alsia Well. Finally, beside an ancient lane running through fields is **Kemyel C** [4587 2458], a 1.7m (5½ft) stone, that is on an alignment to the Castallack stone and Kerris stone.

DRIFT - PAUL AREA

Drift stones [4371/2 2831]. Formerly known as The Sisters, this pair of stones are beside the A30 road - one 2.3m (7½ft), the other 2.7m (9ft), some 5.5m (18ft) apart. Borlase in 1871 found there had been a pit dug between them, which he thought had been a grave. It has been suggested that the 2 stones align precisely with the horizon.4 Leys: [1] Sancreed churchyard & cross - Drift north - Chyenhal - Chapel at Mousehole [2] Drift north - destroyed stone at 4041 2721 - Trevear - Sennen stone. [3] NE Piper -stone in hedge 4360 2585 - stone as gatepost 4365 2710 - Drift stones - Carfury stone. [4] *See* Goldherring *p.36*.

Tresvennack [4418 2788]. A 3.6m (11½ft) high menhir, reached by a footpath from the Drift-Mousehole road. An 1840 dig found 2 urns, now in Penlee Museum. Leys: [1] Tresvennack stone - Trengwainton Cairn cross 4405 3218 - Carfury stone [2] Tresvennack stone - Trenuggo cross 4281 2764 - Boscawen-ûn circle (Circle Ley [1]) [3] Chyangwens stone - Tresvennack stone-Faughan Round stones [4522 2822] [4] Tresvennack stone - Kerris stone - stone in hedge 4510 2597 - Kerris Round - lost stone 4550 2513 - Redhouse stone [5] Tresvennack stone - Blind Fiddler stone - stone at 3908 2884.

There was a second fallen stone nearby to Tresvennack at 4426 2793, which now lies in a lane near the field at 4425 2815.

DRIFT - PAUL AREA [cont.]

Chyenhal [4507 2751] This fine 2.4m (8ft) menhir stands SW of Chyenhal Farm, off the minor road from Drift to Mousehole. There were formerly 2 other stones in the next field at 4491 2745 & 4497 2746 (the latter on Boscawen-ûn Hedge stone Ley [3]). Leys:[1]Sancreed church yard & cross - Drift north - Chyenhal - Mousehole Chapel. [2] Missing stone at Brea 3814 2799 - Boscawen-ûn Hedge stone - Trenuggo cross 4281 2764 - Missing stone 4497 2747 - Cheyenhal. [3] West Lanyon quoit - Ennis Farm stone - Cheyenhal menhir .

Ennis Farm [4475 2821] 2.3m (7½ft) stone in hedge beside Drift-Mousehole road Leys: [1] Chyenhal [3]. [2] Kerris [3].

Sheffield [4585 2752]. 2.4m (8ft) high stone stands in hedge. Leys: [1] Sheffield - NE Piper -Merry Maidens-Boscawen-Ros E [2] Sheffield - Toldavas - Trevorgans.

Kerris [4439 2743] A triangular stone, excavated by Borlase who found only pebble and flint. Nearby is another Round with 2 entrance stones in a wall behind a house [4450 2720]. Leys: [1]Tresvennack- Kerris - Kerris Round [2] Faughan hill fort - Kerris - Treverven [3] Ennis - Kerris - Pipers SW

Redhouse Two stones stand in neighbouring fields: one [4480 2663] is a thin roundish slab; the other [4476 2658] a 2m [6ft] high menhir. The former is on 4 leys: [1] to Boscawen-ûn circle - destroyed Carn Brea stone. [2] Trelew - Redhouse - cross at 4623 2647. [3] Redhouse - Trevorgans - Sennen Hedge [4] Tresvennack Ley (4).

ST. BURYAN AREA

Toldavas [4266 2671] A large erected boulder, found by John Michell following Lockyer's November sunrise line from Boscawen-ûn circle - Trelew - Toldavas - Castallack [Boscawen-ûn circle [3]]. A further ley was found from Trevorgans - Toldavas - Sheffield.

Trevorgans [4047 2614] In a field north of St.Buryan. Leys: [1] Boscawen-ûn circle - Trevorgans - St.Levan cross 3820 2236 [2] Sennen Hedge - Trevorgans - destroyed stone 4152 2626 - destroyed stone circle 4169 2625 -Redhouse [3] Trevorgans - Toldavas - Sheffield.

Pridden [4165 2661] In a field just off the B3315 Penzance-St.Buryan road. Now leaning at an angle, originally upright when excavated by Borlase in 1871. There is a 2m (6ft) stone in the hedge of the road 100 yds south which may have led to a destroyed stone circle at 4169 2659. Trelew menhir is visible on horizon.

A mile south of St.Buryan, near to Selena Farm is a field where 2 menhirs formerly stood at 3974 2399, until removed some time after 1842. One of these stones was over 3m (9ft 10in) high, and remains of it can be seen in the field hedge.

14

Trelew [4217 2693] Standing just off the B3283 Penzance-St.Buryan road, this is a 3m (10ft) menhir excavated in 1872 by Borlase, who found a pit 3ft away containing pieces of wood, flint, clay and bone.
Leys: [1] Boscawen-ûn circle Ley [3]
[2] Trelew - Redhouse - cross 4623 2647 -Mousehole ancient chapel 4693 2639
[3] Trelew - Boscawen-ûn hedge stone - destroyed barrow 3906 3260
[4] Tregeseal circle - Trelew - NE Piper
[5] Newham farm-Trelew-Boscawen-RosW

Chyangwens [4186 2709]. Stone in hedge on Ley to Tresvennack - Faughan Round stone (Tresvennack Ley [3]). Some doubts were expressed about its provenance, but John Michell pointed out *[in Meyn Mamvro no.8]* that it is the only erected earthfast stone in the hedge. Nearby at 4182 2707 is a buried fallen longstone, which if standing would be on a 5 point alignment from Boscawen-ûn circle [Circle Ley [3]].

Blind Fiddler [4252 2818] Standing in a field just north of the A30 Penzance - Lands End road, this is a fine 3.3m (10¾ft) high menhir. Ley: Tresvennack - Blind Fiddler - stone at 3908 2884. There is also a visual alignment from a stone at Trenuggo Farm [4265 2782] to the Blind Fiddler and on to the top of Sancreed Beacon. Hamish Miller found spiral energy patterns at this stone clockwise at waxing moon & anticlockwise at waning. Anomalous earthsound experienced here at summer solstice sunset in 1987.

Boscawen-ûn Field [4149 2761] Three fields to the NE of the circle is this 2.6m (8½ft) menhir, which Lockyer thought had been set to mark the rise of the star Capella in 2250 BCE. Leys: [1] Boscawen-ûn Field - Boscawen-ûn circle - stone at 3978 2594

[2] Boscawen-ûn Hedge - Boscawen-ûn Field - Trevear - Sennen. Another menhir which may once have stood nearby is now built lengthways into the hedge.

Boscawen-ûn Hedge [4174 2770] In the lane leading to the farm from the A30 road is a triangular pointed stone (with another on the opposite side of the lane, visible from the field).

Leys: [1] Field stone [2] above. [2]Trelew - Boscawen-ûn Hedge - destroyed barrow 3906 3260. [3] Destroyed Chapel Carn Brea stone - Boscawen-ûn Hedge - Trenuggo cross 4281 2764

There were formerly 2 other stones to the west of Boscawen-ûn circle at 4041 2721 & 4031 2719, forming an alignment with the circle, noted by John Michell in 1974 but since destroyed by the farmer.

SANCREED AREA
Newham Farm [4172 2916] 1.95m (6¼ft) stone in hedge. Leys: [1] Boscawen-ûn circle - Newham farm - Lanyon Quoit - Boskednan outlier [2] Newham farm - Trelew - Boscawen-Ros west [3] Tregeseal entrance - Newham farm - Redhouse [4] Newham farm - Castallack - Swingate.

15

NEWBRIDGE AREA
[Off A3071 Penzance - St Just road]

Tremayne [4298 3136] (called 'Trewern' in John Michell's 'Old Stones of Lands End'). South of the main road behind the farm. One stone remains out of an original pair, the other destroyed around 1900. Borlase dug between them in 1752 and found a pit like Drift, but no burial. No Leys noted.

Trewern [4320 3208] North of the main road, again behind a farm. Again, one stone remains out of an original pair, the other (at 4319 3194) destroyed c.1958 They stood near Trewern Round *[p.47]*, which also has 2 entrance stones (1 in situ), as at Kerris Round & Faughan Round hill fort *[p.45]*. No Leys.

SENNEN/LANDS END AREA
Sennen hedge [3546 2557]. Overlooking the sea towards Lands End, this stone stands isolated and distant from other clus-

ters of menhirs, but is at the terminus of several good leys:
[1] Sennen - tumulus 3725 2774 - edge of barrow 4032 3141 - crossroads 4061 3175 - West Lanyon Quoit - Nine Maidens circle [2] Sennen - Trevear - destroyed stone 4041 2721 - Drift north [3] Sennen - Trevorgans - vanished stone 4152 2626 - Redhouse [4] Boscawen-ûn Field [2]. Some suggestion that the stone may have been moved (1870 map marks different position) but this is disputed.

Trevear (Sennen) This triangular stone was formerly at 3685 2598 in a field to the east of Sennen, but was uprooted in 1972 by the farmer and dumped in the hedge. Originally on 2Leys to Sennen hedge stone
Chapel Carn Brea Another stone destroyed in 1972, this one in a field to the west of Chapel Carn Brea at 3814 2799. Originally on 3 Leys: Boscawen-ûn Hedge [3]; Boscawen-ûn Circle [7]; Carfury [3]. Another stone in wall nearby at 3867 2847

WEST PENWITH MOORS
Boswens [4001 3290] 2.5m (8½ft) stone, near Dry Carn (path off the B3318 Pen-

deen North Road) - variously shaped on different sides. The tip of the stone is visible from Tregeseal Circle [Ley [1] below], and is intervisible with Chûn Quoit.
It was originally surrounded by a low cairn, and in 1987 snowfalls, the cairn area was free from snow, perhaps indicating some 'hot spot' there. There are reported instances of animals being reluctant to enter the area. Leys: [1] Tregeseal stone circle - Boswens - West Lanyon Quoit - Mulfra Courtyard House settlement (Beltane sunrise line)
[2] Boswens - Nine Maidens circle - line of boundary stones [3] Boswens - tumulus 4324 3530 - stone 4448 3623 - Zennor Quoit - cairn on Trendrine Hill 4787 3871.

At the foot of **Dry Carn** beside the B3318 road is a 3m (10ft) standing stone, found in field & re-erected in hedge 4025 3185.
At **Trevean Farm** near Morvah, the Trevowhan menhir [4089 3513] was uprooted some time after 1975 & now lies in corner of the field (plans to re-erect it).

Watch Croft [4209 3567] On the brow of the hill next to Carn Gulva, reachable by a pathway from the B3306 north coast road, or by one from Madron-Morvah road. May be aligned to a notch in Carn Gulva at May dawn.

Men Scryfa [4268 3529] A 1.8m (6ft) high stone, probably Bronze Age in origin, but inscribed in the Iron Age with the lettering RIALO-BRANI CVNOVALI FILI (the last word below ground), meaning "Rigalo-branus, son of Cunoualos". The first name means "royal raven" and is linked to the name of the Celtic God Bran. The stone is aligned to a distinctive notch in Carn Gulva, at what may be the northerly standstill of the moon, and there is a Ley to a tumulus at 4324 3540 - Mulfra Quoit.

Porthmeor [4325 3726]. A 1.8m (6ft) high standing stone, overlooking the sea near a settlement off the B3306 St.Just - St.Ives road. There was an early 20th century reference by Henderson to it being an "inscribed stone" but no trace of this now remains. It was excavated in 1879 but no finds were made.

Kerrow [4524 3733] A 1.8m (6ft) high stone, standing at back of farm. Excavated 1935 when 2 urns were discovered.

Carfury [4400 3400] A lovely setting for this largely unknown 3m (10ft) stone, standing in a low hedge, hidden off a minor road to Ding Dong mine, or reachable from Newmill - Carfury road below. Excavated in 1958 but no finds. It stands at the terminus of 5 separate leys, and also on 2 others, more than any other stone in West Penwith: [1] stone 4788 3764 - Bishops Head & Foot boundary stone 4638 3623 - Carfury [2] Sennen church - tumulus 3745 2728 - Destroyed Ch.Carn Brea stone - Stone in wall at Ch.Carn Brea - Bartinney Castle cairn - tumulus4138 3131 - Carfury [3] NE Piper - stone 4360 2585 - gatepost 4365 2710 - Drift stones - Carfury [4] Tresvennack - Trengwainton Cairn cross - Carfury [5] cairn4190 3545 - Mên-an-Tol - Bosiliack stone- Carfury [6] Tregeseal Circle Ley (3) [7] tumulus 4699 3610 - Mulfra Vean Courtyard House settlement - Carfury- 3 boundary stones- tumulus 4032 3141.

Bosiliack [4369 3423] In hedge of lane to Ding Dong mine, 1.8m (5¾ft). Leys: [1] Carfury Ley[5] [2] Boswarthen cross - Boswarthen - Bosiliack - Carn Gulva
Boswarthen [4428 3301] A boulder stone, possibly stump of a menhir. Originally in nearby hedge at 4427 3298.
Try [4597 3498] 2.8m (9ft) high menhir standing in Try farm. Excavated 1958 & 1962 - stone cist with large capstone containing beaker, pottery & bones found.

1 -Pipers 2 - Gûn Rith 3 - Boscawen-Ros
4 - Treverven 5 - Castallack 6 - Castallack Carn
7 - Swingate 8 - Kemyel 9 - Drift
10 - Tresvennack 11 - Kerris 12 - Chyenhal
13 Ennis Farm 14 - Sheffield 15 - Redhouse
16 - Pridden 17 - Trelew 18 - Toldavas
19 - Trevorgans
20 = Chyangwens

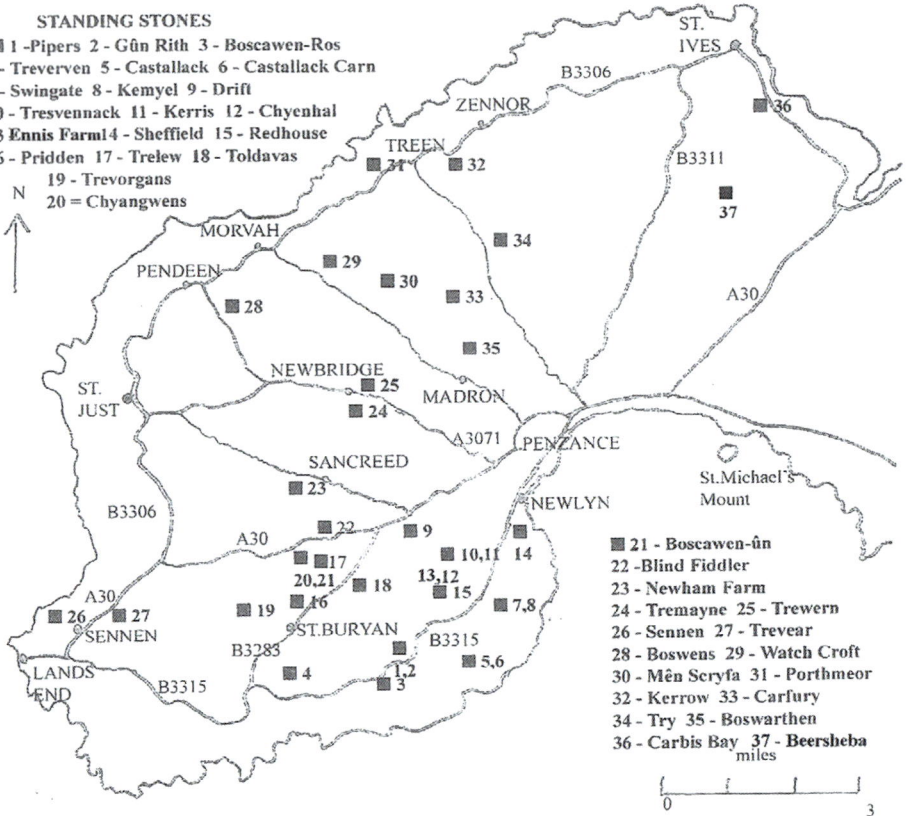

21 - Boscawen-ûn
22 - Blind Fiddler
23 - Newham Farm
24 - Tremayne 25 - Trewern
26 - Sennen 27 - Trevear
28 - Boswens 29 - Watch Croft
30 - Mên Scryfa 31 - Porthmeor
32 - Kerrow 33 - Carfury
34 - Try 35 - Boswarthen
36 - Carbis Bay 37 - Beersheba

miles
0   3

ST.IVES/CARBIS BAY AREA
St.Ives Carnello stone [5056 4016] remains behind Rugby Club. **Carbis Bay** Longstone [5303 3821] next to a bus stop.

TRENCROM HILL AREA
Beersheba [5251 3714]. A fine 3m (10ft) standing stone on the St.Michaels Way in a field north of Trencrom Hill *[see p.46]*. Remote from other standing stones, but has an equinox sunset alignment over the Twelve O'Clock rock on neighbouringTrink Hill, and an energy line running on to Carn Brea.

STONE ROWS
There are few authenticated stone rows in West Penwith, but one possibility is the **Zennor Stone Row.** At one end [4528 3891] there is a stone in a hedge, with a further two stones in the field, one of which is standing and the other fallen. The row then continues in an ESE direction to a large 2.5m (8½ft) stone at 4539 3887 now used as a gatepost *[photo above]*. This stone forms a perfect visual alignment with the top of Trendrine Hill (with possible entrance grave- *see p.30*) in the direction of the Imbolc/Samhain (Feb/Nov) sunrise.

CONCLUSIONS

As the preceding pages show, there are a great number and variety of standing stones in West Penwith. What then was their purpose? There are a number of different possibilities, not all mutually exclusive. One suggestion is that they were markers for graves of important people. Some evidence for this can be found at the Try menhir *[right]*, which appeared to mark a cist grave. There is also the possible evidence of the urns found at Kerrow and Tresvennack menhirs, and the bones and ashes found at Pridden and the Blind Fiddler. However, these could equally well have been foundation offerings to the stone, rather than the stone marking the burial. Not all standing stones have been excavated, and of those that have, many were done in the early days of archaeology, so much vital evidence may have been destroyed. But nevertheless Try is the only menhir to have yielded a proper cist burial, and even in this case the cist grave had been dug *after* the erection of the standing stone and was separate from it, so grave markers seems an unlikely explanation.

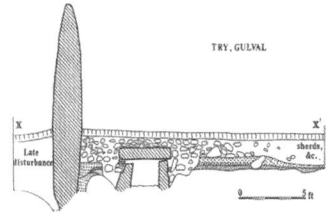

A second possibility is that they were markstones for important tribal leaders or events; there is the legend that the Pipers marked the site of a battle, and the Men Scryfa is inscribed with the name of Rialobran. But both the inscription and the legend date to several thousand years after the stones themselves were erected, and appear to be a later gloss on a stone whose original purpose had been forgotten.

A study by the archaeologist Frances Peters *[Cornish Archaeology, 29, 1990]* suggested that the menhirs were purposely positioned along contours on the upper parts of slopes to be seen from other menhirs, in order to mark boundaries between groups of people. However, a total of over 100 menhirs which used to be extant in West Penwith seems very excessive for merely boundary markers. The research also revealed that a total of 73 out of 95 menhirs or menhir sites would have been intervisible from another menhir or menhir site. However, this intervisibility need not have denoted boundary divisions. It could equally be an argument for sacred trackways or leypaths stretching across the land. Williams *[British Archaeology, 3, 1988]* suggested that standing stones were features of overwhelming ritual significance, and that burial was only one aspect of some ceremonial activity. If this is so, then part of that ritual significance may have included the positioning of the stone because it stood in relationship to some particular landscape feature, or at the borderline between perceived sacred land areas, or even because the ancestors had lived there, or had previously used the site. It may also have been positioned to observe astronomical events as part of a pattern of earth and cosmic magic, with the stones set up as outliers to circles, or in alignment with each other across the landscape (leys?). There were probably foundation offerings at the site of special pebbles or quartzite pieces, perhaps thought of as gifts from or to Mother Earth, The stone may have been decorated or thought of as being 'alive' in some magical way. Whatever their precise meaning, they were certainly sacred points in the land of our ancestors.

holed stones & stone rows

MÊN-AN-TOL

The Mên-an-Tol [4264 3493](Cornish for 'Stone of the Hole') consists of a holed stone 1.2m (4ft) across with a large round hole 51cm (20 in) in diameter, large enough for a grown person to crawl through. Either side of it are two upright stones, 1.3m (4½ft) high. There is also a fallen stone, and leading away around the edge the visible remains of other stones.

The setting of the holed stone and two uprights was first drawn by William Borlase in 1754, although according to his plan, they were not in a straight line, but on "a triangular plan". This indicates that at least one of the stones (the centre or one of the uprights) has since then been moved to its present position. This may not have been the first time it has been moved. When they cleared the site some years ago, the Cornwall Archaeological Unit suggested that what can be seen today are the remains of a stone circle, which probably originally consisted of 19 stones (as do the other circles in West Penwith) with traces of 11 stone stumps still visible. It is not clear where the holed stone fitted into this circle. It may have formed the entrance to a small burial chamber abutting on to the circle: there appears to be the remains of a small stone mound next to the holed stone, which could have been the base of a small chamber. There are no other known sites such as this in Cornwall, but similar sites have been recorded in places such as Gloucestershire in England, and in France and Belgium. Alternatively, the holed stone could have been set at the edge of the circle, either freestanding, or indeed on top of the mound if there was one (some burial mounds in Britanny had standing stones on top of them, and Newgrange in Ireland may also have done). The CAU had suggested that the stone was originally at right angles to its present position with the hole facing out of the circle, so *Meyn Mamvro* ran some computer alignments for 2000 BCE & 1800 BCE, and discovered that an observer in the centre of the circle would have seen the moon rise over a barrow to the NE of the circle at the northern major standstill. Furthermore, at the southern major standstill moonrise the moon would have been seen to rise above the horizon and be framed perfectly by the holed stone itself - a wonderful piece of megalithic magic!

The holed stone has long been the subject of legends relating to healing and divination. Formerly known as the Crick stone, it was thought that to crawl through the hole nine times widdershins (against the sun or anti-clockwise) was a cure for backache, rickets and scrofula. Children would be passed through three times. Also, if a brass pin was placed on the stone, questions could be answered by the movement of the pin. It has also been suggested that the stone could have served as a means of passing through the bones of the dead ancestors for use in fertility rituals, and that the stone could have provided a symbolic 'rebirthing' for the people at various 'rites of passage' in their lives.

There is another round holed stone in the hedge of the lane opposite the entrance to the Mên-an-Tol at 4242 3499, 1.1m (3¾ft) diameter with 0.15m (6in) diameter hole.

HOLED STONES AT THE MERRY MAIDENS

A number of holed stones with relatively small holes are, or were, near the Merry Maidens stone circle, several of which form a straight alignment over 1200 metres (1300 yds). The 6 point alignment runs from [1] a holed stone in a hedge at Bosacwen-Ros at 4277 2421 which is 1.1m (3¾ft) high, 1m (3½ft) wide & 0.3m (1ft) thick, with a hole 0.25m (10in) in diameter, to [2] Tregiffian EntranceGrave with its cupmarked stones *[p.27]*, to [3] the remains of a holed stone in the ground at 4315 2450, to [4] a holed stone used as a gatepost 4324 2457, to [5] Nun Careg cross (slightly off the line) at 4329 2460, to [6] a (partial) holed stone in the wall of a farm at 4365 2489. The 4 holed stones are on an azmuth close to the midwinter moonrise at its most northerly extreme, which happens once every 18.6 years, a megalithic calendar which may relate to the number of stones (19) at the Merry Maidens stone circle. There was formerly (in the 1750s) another holed stone called Mên Frith in Rosemodross Lane [4360 2458] to the NE of the Merry Maidens. By 1854 it had been incorporated into a hedge and drawn by Blight. When the hedge was cleared in the 1960s, the stone was moved to Tregurnow farm, about ½ mile away, at 4432 2415.

TREGESEAL HOLED STONES [3895 3255]

These holed stones are similar in many ways to the Merry Maidens ones, being about the same size, in a direct line, and close to a stone circle (although the Tregeseal ones are much closer together). In both cases we many have the remains of an ancient ceremonial site. The Tregeseal (Kenijack Common) stones consist of a straight line of 3 standing and 1 fallen and broken stone, with another, which was probably

originally part of the row, a few yards to the NW. The stones are about 1-1.4m (3-4½ft) high, with bevelled-edge holes all about 8cm (3in) in diameter. Some 90m (100 yds) away to the NE on the hillside is another one with a larger hole with smooth edges of about 0.2m (7in), which may or may not be connected to the row. The stones had fallen and broken when they were cemented together and re-erected by a local farmer in the early 1980s, so we cannot be sure of their original orientation, but they may have been aligned to view the tip of Boswens menhir (4001 3290) on the horizon.

BURIAL CHAMBERS

Cromlechs, dolmens, quoits, entrance graves, chambered tombs, barrows. Stone chambers that are found all over West Penwith, places for the dead - and the living. Strange places standing sentinel on the high moors, or tucked in the corner of a field. Some denuded of their earth coverings, they stand gaunt and stark against the primitive landscape; others covered in with earth mounds lie hidden and secretive, awaiting discovery. There are three main sorts: the cromlechs (Cornish for "curved place"), otherwise known as dolmens called colloqually 'quoits' after the giants of old who hurled their capstones around while playing the ancient game. Then there are the entrance graves, otherwise known as chambered tombs, where people's remains were communally buried. And finally the barrows, with or without burial remains, often positioned dramatically in the landscape.

To crawl into Chapel Carn Brea and see the full moon rise over the hill, framed by the entrance of the barrow, is a moment of pure magic. To stand in Carn Gluze and look out over the Atlantic ocean, watching the sun set beyond the Scillies is a momemt of pure peace. To stand at Mulfra Quoit and watch the sun rise over the Penwith hills until it illuminates the whole of Mounts Bay and St.Michael's Mount before the mist descends is a moment of absolute joy. And to climb the hill at Chûn to the Quoit to see the summer sun set red in the sea one side and the pink full moon rise over the tip of the Lizard at the other, is a moment of complete integration. So must our ancestors have seen all these things, thousands of years ago at these sacred sites.

So why are the sites so sacred? Perhaps because they were tombs for the dead, and their spirits still linger around them sometimes in the Celtic twilight. They may have been built as houses in which the spirits of the dead would continue to live for a very long time. To the ancient peoples, there was no division between the physical and the spiritual, and death was viewed as part of the continuation of life. The dead were there to be talked to, their wisdom to be drawn on by the shamans, their presence to sit over the fields and dwellings of their descendants. It is in these places that we can sense the continuity of a very ancient life in the land of West Penwith. Listen to them and they will speak to you still.

CROMLECHS/DOLMENS/QUOITS

LANYON [4298 3369]. Probably the most accessible and well photographed of all the Quoits, and unfortunately the least authentic! It collapsed in a storm in 1815 and some of the stones were fractured, so that when it was re-erected in 1824 (at right angles to its original position) the capstone was placed on only 3 lower uprights instead of the probable original rectangular box chamber. It is located on relatively low-lying land close to Lanyon Farm, beside the Penzance-Madron-Morvah road. It originally dated from the early Neolithic period (3500-2500 BCE) and consisted of a large capstone 5.3m (17½ft) long and 2.7m (9ft) wide on 4 upright support stones. It stood at the northern end of a burial mound 27m (90ft) long and 12m (40ft) broad, the outline of which is still visible. At the southern end is a collection of stones which may originally have formed a small chamber or cist. In the 18thC Dr.Borlase dug at the site and reported that between the support stones, he had found a grave containing 'black earth'. John Barnett said that it appeared to have continued in use for some time and formed a focal point for later ceremonial activity, and John Michell claimed a ley ran through it from Tregeseal Circle and on to Carfury menhir and Chysauster Courtyard House settlement.

WEST LANYON [4231 3379]. This ruined Quoit lies about ½ mile from Lanyon Quoit, in a sloping field to the south of the road. There is no public access to this site and permission to visit it should be sought from Lanyon Farm. In 1790 a mound in this field was cleared and the remains of this Quoit were discovered. It consists of a fallen capstone 4.2m (13ft) long by 3.2m (10½ft) wide propped up against one upright stone, with another broken one underneath. Most other extant Quoits are some distance from each other, as though they were marking tribal boundaries, so the close proximity of Lanyon & West Lanyon is curious (though Zennor & Sperris are also close to each other). Large deposits of bones were found when it was discovered, and possibly bronze and copper objects as well. John Michell claimed 2 leys: [1] Tregeseal circle - Boswens menhir - West Lanyon Quoit - Mulfra Courtyard House settlement, marking the Beltane sunrise. [2] Nine Maidens circle - West Lanyon Quoit - crossroads 4061 3175 - barrow edge 4032 3141 - tumulus 3725 2774 - Sennen hedge menhir.

Giant's Grave, Morvah. Thurston Hopkins, writing in the 1930s, makes mention of a ruined cromlech called "The Giant's Grave" near Morvah Church, and adds "People still living can remember the rites at the grave for gaining knowledge of the future. Most of the Giants Grave has been removed for mending roads". Part of the stone may still be found at the corner of an ancient track running from the church to the coast at 4034 3567.

CHÛN [4023 3396]. Chûn Quoit (pronounced *Choon*) lies on a high spot on the West Penwith moors near to Pendeen. It can be seen clearly on the horizon from the B3318 road that runs from Portherras Cross at Pendeen to join the A3071 road to Penzance. The site can be reached from three directions. One from Keigwin near Pendeen by a public footpath, one from the B3318 road, where there is a small car-parking area and a permissive path that climbs up to the hill, and one from Trehyllys Farm to Chûn Castle. It is the only Quoit still almost prfectly preserved. The monument consists of a closed chamber of four slabs 1.5m (4ft) high which lean inwards and support a convex capstone 3.7m (12ft) square and up to 0.8m (2½ft) thick., and is surrounded by a low circular mound which is probably the remains of a former barrow, which however may not have completely covered the capstone. There is a cupmark on top of the capstone. The midwinter solstice sun sets in a notch over Carn Kenidjack when viewed from the Quoit, and a strong energy line has been detected running from the hill top (Chûn Castle) through the Quoit and on to the notch in Carn Kenidjack. There is also a good visual alignment from Portheras Common entrance grave, through a possible standing stone now used as a gatepost (3980 3360) to the Quoit. Anomalous multicoloured lights were observed running over the Quoit by archaeologist John Barnatt in 1979. Paul Devereux commented that the high radioactive count of the Quoit (123% higher than environment) may be related to this event.

MULFRA [4518 3536]. Originally this site must have resembled Chûn, standing in the centre of a circular barrow, near the top of a hill with fine views over West Penwith. The 2.9m (9½ft) square capstone, weighting 5 tons, has slipped off the box chamber and now leans against 2 of the remaining 3 uprights. It too has a possible cupmark on the upperside of the capstone. Borlase dug within, and, as at Lanyon, found a pit containing black earth. A ley runs from here to a boundary stone, a tumulus at 4324 3530, and on to the Mên Scryfa stone.

GRUMBLA [4049 2955]. The remains of this quoit can be found in a sloping field at Caer Bran farm. It was thought to have been destroyed around 1840, but in fact is still quite well preserved, consisting of a large upright stone some 3m (10ft) wide at base & 1.8m (6ft) high, which could have been the original capstone. 5m (17ft) away there is another upright, 1.2m (4ft) wide & 1.4m (4½ft) high. Other broken stones lie about, some of which may have been used as a dwelling in historical times.

ZENNOR [4688 3801]. A path from Eagles Nest on the B3306 road above Zennor leads up to this Quoit, high on the remote Penwith moors. Two large facade stones form an ante-chamber to the monument, which may have been used for rituals. The chamber behind is 2.4m (8ft) high, and the whole structure once stood within a barrow 12.8m (42ft) in diameter. The capstone is 5.5m (18ft) long, 2.9m (9½ft) wide and weighs 9.3 tons, and now leans back-wards over the chamber, the result of some collapse of a support, clearance by a farmer, and blasting in the 19thC. Stones standing to the E of the monument are the remains of a more modern (19th C) cow shed. Finds include a whetstone and some pottery with cord impressions, which tends to support the theory that the tombs may have been used for rituals, perhaps to honour the dead ancestors. A recent radiocarbon date for the site places it at 3342-3024 BCE. This was the place where the Cornish Earth Mysteries Group heard the enigmatic 'hummadruz' sound in 1997. One Ley runs from Boswens menhir - tumulus 4324 3530 - stone 4448 3623 - Zennor Quoit - parish boundary - Trendrine Hill cairn.

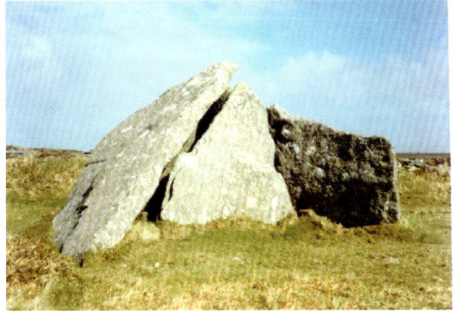

SPERRIS [4709 3826]. Also known as Tregerthen or Giants Rock, this Quoit was re-discovered and excavated in the 1950s. It lies only 370m (400yds) NE of Zennor Quoit, and can be found by following a path running E from ruined mine buildings, over Sperris Carn. It is much smaller than Zennor Quoit, with only 1 upright and 3 fallen stones remaining. The cap-stone is missing, but it may originally have had a south-facing antechamber. Excavation revealed a small cremation pit just outside the chamber, itself lying in the low remains of an oval barrow. A recent radiocarbon date for the site places it at 3633-3557 BCE, at the very beginning of the Neolithic period, and earlier than its bigger neighbour, Zennor Quoit.

BOSPORTHENNIS [4356 3654]. This hard-to-find site consists of three out of four upright chamber stones embedded in an oval mound. The capstone, now fallen, is unusually thin and was possibly trimmed for use as a millstone in the past. The site was excavated in 1872, when sherds of pottery and calcinated bones were found, and again in 2009 when knapped flint and a leaf-shaped arrow-head were found. It is in a low lying position at a valley bottom, which is unusual for a Quoit, and it has been suggested recently that it may in fact be the remains of an Entrance Grave rather than a Quoit.

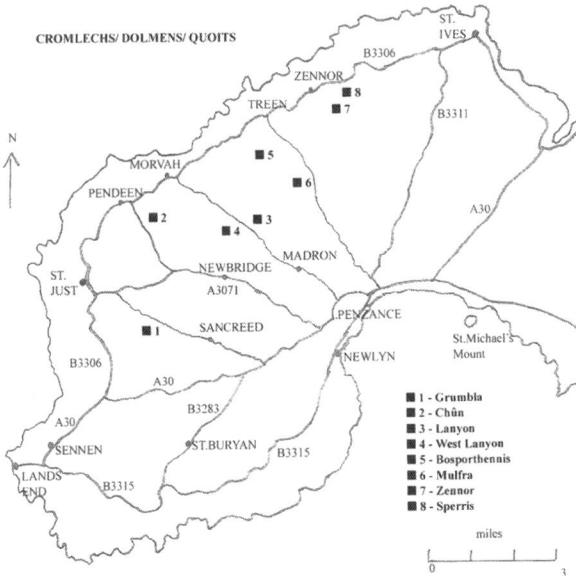

CROMLECHS/ DOLMENS/ QUOITS

1 - Grumbla
2 - Chûn
3 - Lanyon
4 - West Lanyon
5 - Bosporthennis
6 - Mulfra
7 - Zennor
8 - Sperris

miles

OTHER SITES

Trewey Cromlech, Zennor
Edmonds in 1857 mentions a destroyed cromlech at Trewey near Zennor. This may or may not be the same as The Witches Rock, a natural boulder stone.

Giants Rock, Towednack
Borlase mentions a cromlech destroyed in 1702. Hoard of Roman coins was found.

Hewas an Quoit (Field of the Quoit). 2 field names in St. Just, one at Bosavern and one at Carrallack, indicate the presence of former megaliths which may have been cromlechs.

CONCLUSIONS

There are a number of quoits (approximately 8 remaining) found usually (though not always) on high ground throughout West Penwith. Interestingly, they are often near, but not on, the tops of hills, and this may relate to the importance for the builders to be able to see the monument from their settlements below. These sites were clearly non-utiliterian, and probably were designed as repositories for the bones of the dead, whose bodies may have been laid out on the capstones for the carrion birds to remove the flesh (a practice known as excarnation). Yet it would be a mistake to think of these monuments simply as 'burial chambers'. The bone evidence from cromlechs in other places indicates that the disarticulated bones of a number of individuals may have been placed inside, and from time to time some bones were removed and were replaced by others. We may perhaps rather think of these sites as places where the tribe (or the shamans of the tribe) would go to consult with the spirits of their dead ancestors in trance journeys and altered states of consciousness.

These sites date from the earliest period of settlement in West Penwith, when the Mesolithic foraging tribes began to settle down in the land and graze herds of animals and plant crops. They then had the time, energy and resources to build these Quoits, which were clearly places of ceremonial significance, standing on the hill slopes outside the living areas. Quoits existed before the stone circles were built, before the standing stones were erected, and before the entrance graves and barrows came into fashion. They are the earliest megalithic monuments, and may be some of the first places for ceremonial communion with the spirits of the ancestors. Fires were probably lit outside them, and the dead would be honoured regularly by giving offerings to the tombs, and by communion with the spirits of the dead. These places were not mausoleums where the dead were locked away: rather they were the dwelling places of the spirits of the ancestors of the tribes. The living and the dead inhabited the same world in the dolmens and quoits.

ENTRANCE GRAVES/CHAMBERED TOMBS

TREGIFFIAN [4303 2442] Situated near the Merry Maidens stone circle on the south grass verge of the road. Part of the kerb remains as do some roofing stones, one of which is 3.4m (11ft) long, and which looks like a re-used menhir. Another roofing stone has a cupmark on top, and other cupmarked stones were found inside during a 1967 excavation. The eastern entrance stone (original in Truro Museum & replica on site) was inscribed with 13 cupmarks and 12 ovals, which Ian Cooke has suggested were intended to represent the 12 new or full moons & 13 full or new moons of the lunar year. The stone was originally pointing *inwards* to the tomb, showing that it was intended to be seen by the dead. The barrow has a radiocarbon date of 1995-1680 BCE, taken from charcoal with a pot that which was probably placed there at a later date than the construction of the monement. Dimensions: 8m (26ft) in diameter, with the chamber 4.3m (14ft) long, 1.2m (4ft) wide & 0.9m (3ft) high. Orientation of entrance is 110° (just S of E). An alignment runs through several holed stones in the area and touches the edge of the grave, on an azimuth of 45° 47', very close to the midwinter moonrise at its northerly extreme, once every 18.6 years, a megalithic calendar which may relate to the number of stones (19) at the Merry Maidens stone circle.

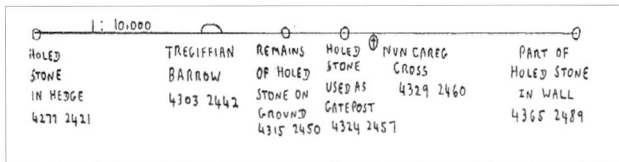

1: 10,000					
HOLED STONE IN HEDGE 4277 2421	TREGIFFIAN BARROW 4303 2442	REMAINS OF HOLED STONE ON GROUND 4315 2450	HOLED STONE USED AS GATEPOST 4324 2457	NUN CAREG CROSS 4329 2460	PART OF HOLED STONE IN WALL 4365 2489

Lockyer also calculated that an alignment between Merry Maidens circle - Tregiffian Barrow - Boskenna cross [4255 2427] - Boskenna Gate cross [4201 2407], denoted the Antares constellation in 1310 BCE, which would have warned of the May Day sunrise.

BRANE [4014 2818]. This is a small beautiful grave of simple construction lying in the corner of a field to the SW of Brane Farm (ask permission). The passage is well preserved with its opening on the SSE side, and has 2 large roof slabs still in place. The small round kerb cairn has 7 blocks remaining. Dimensions: 6.1m (20ft) in diameter & 2m (6½ft) tall. Chamber: 2.3m (7½ft) long, 1.2m (4ft) wide & 0.9m (3ft) high. Orientation of entrance: 155° (SSE), major southern moonrise?). Leys [1] Brane - Bosiliack - Pennance graves [2] *Goldherring p.36*

TREGIFFIAN VEAN [3725 2771]. The remains of an entrance grave can be found in a field near the sea between St.Just & Sennen. It was excavated by W.C.Borlase in 1858 when ashes & an urn were found. Now all that remains is a short passage and capstone.

CHAPEL CARN BREA [3859 2807].
Situated on the top of the 'first and last hilltop'
in Britain, this site has a long and complex
history. First to be built in the late Neolithic
was a chambered cairn 9m (29ft) in diameter
containing a S facing chamber. This was subsequently covered by a huge cairn 19m (62ft)
across & 4.6m (15ft) high, containing 3 concentric retaining walls and a secondary cist. In the
13thC a tiny hermitage chapel of St.Michael of
Brea was built on top of the cairn, but this was demolished in 1816 after falling into decay.
W.C.Borlase dug the site in 1868 & 1879 and a new cairn was built, but this was destroyed
by a WWII radar observation post (itself now gone). Dimensions of entrance grave: 2.7m
(8¾ft) long, 1.1m (3½ft) wide & 1.2m (4ft) high. Orientation of entrance 157° which faces
the major southern moonrise at the standstill (which was confirmed by observation in 1987)

CARN GLUZE (BALLOWAL) [3555
3124]. This chambered tomb lies 1 mile west
of St.Just beside a minor road that leads off the
road to Cape Cornwall. It faces out over a
dramatic seascape towwards the Isles of Scilly,
but has been much disturbed by W.C.Borlase's
excavations in 1878. The entrance grave with 2
capstones (orginally 4 or 5) is on the SW side,
and was probably built before the huge barrow
(about 11.2m (37ft) in diameter and originally
roofed) was constructed around it. The barrow
also contained 2 cists. Dimensions of entrance grave: 3.3m (11ft) long, 1.7m (5½ft) wide &
0.9m (3ft) high. Orientation of entrance: 187° (south). Chapel Carn Brea is visible from this
site, and at the southern standstill of 2006 the moon was observed to rise over the site of
Chapel Carn Brea from this site. Traditions here of lights seen with fairies dancing around
by miners in the 19thC, perhaps evidence of earth lights caused by underground fault lines.

TREGESEAL [3805 3213]. Situated in a field on the
west side of Tregeseal valley, this chambered cairn has a
large oval mound 12.5m (40ft) x 9.4m (30ft), with about
a third of its kerb remaining. The chambered cairn has 2
capstones remaining in place. Dimensions: 3.3m (10ft)
long, 1.2m (4ft) wide. Orientation of entrance: 127°
(SE), the direction of the midwinter solstice sunrise.
Excavated in 1879 by W.C.Borlase who found a cist,
containing a large urn. On Tregeseal Circle ley [1].
*There may also be the remains of another entrance
grave to the NE of Tregeseal circle at 3891 3258.*

BOSILIACK [4311 3422]. This site lies north of Lanyon Quoit, about ¼ mile off the Madron-Morvah road. It sits in a terrace not far from a settlement of 10 round houses (at 428 344). Excavated in 1984 when it was discovered that fertile soil had been deliberately laid on the floor of the chamber when built, and a pot deposited containing partly-cremated bone, all of which may have been intended to be a ritual offering associated with the fertility of the land.

Barrow: 5.1m (16½ft) diameter, 1.1m (3½ft) high. Dimensions of entrance grave: 1.5m (4¾ft) long, 0.7m (2¼ft) wide. Orientation of entrance: 135° (midwinter solstice sunrise). Ley runs through 3 entrance graves: Brane - Bosiliack Barrow - Pennance.

TREEN COMMON South [4384 3711] **North** [4381 3715]. There are 4 barrows here of which 2 are recognisable as entrance graves. They lie in adjoining fields on the west side of the Penzance-Gurnards Head road.

Treen South is the better preserved of the two, with a mound 7.6m (25ft) across. Dimensions of entrance grave: 4m (13ft) long, 1.2m (4ft) wide & 0.9m (3ft) high. Orientation of entrance: 348° (NW, the midsummer solstice sunset, or perhaps the major northern moonset at standstill).

Treen South

Treen North is more overgrown and difficult of access. The mound is 6m (19½ft), and the entrance grave is has only the inner end of the chamber and one capstone remaining. Its orientation though is spot on: 220°, denoting the midwinter solstice sunset.

PENNANCE [4476 3753]. This well-preserved entrance grave lies ¾mile west of Zennor on the St.Ives-St.Just B3306 road. It can be seen clearly from the road lying in a field at Pennance Farm (ask permission) and is known locally as the 'The Giant's Craw'. The mound (8m or 26ft in diameter) is retained by a kerb of alternate large and small granite stones, and is roofed with 5 capstones. Dimensions of entrance grave: 4m (13ft) long, 1.4m (4½ft) wide & 0.8m

(2½ft) high. Orientation of entrance: 110°, the same as Tregiffian Entrance Grave, near Merry Maidens. Ley runs through 3 entrance graves: Brane - Bosiliack Barrow - Pennance.

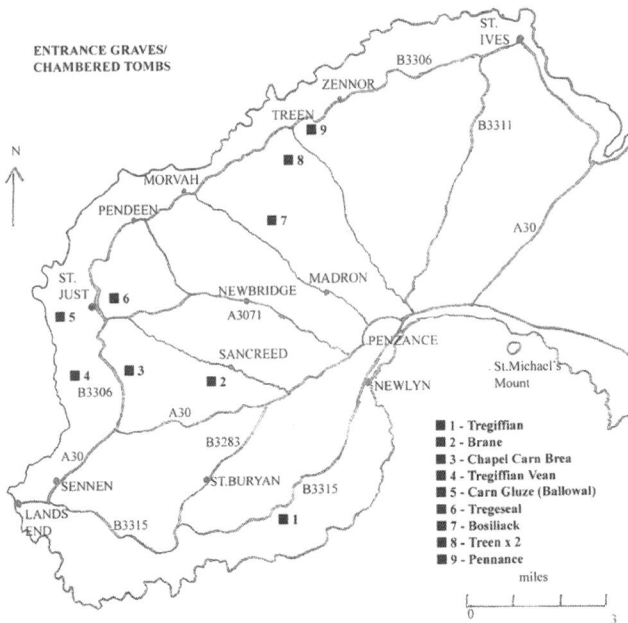

ENTRANCE GRAVES/
CHAMBERED TOMBS

■ 1 - Tregiffian
■ 2 - Brane
■ 3 - Chapel Carn Brea
■ 4 - Tregiffian Vean
■ 5 - Carn Gluze (Ballowal)
■ 6 - Tregeseal
■ 7 - Bosiliack
■ 8 - Treen x 2
■ 9 - Pennance

miles
0   3

OTHER SITES

Pordenack Point, nr. Land's End [3468 2418]. A possible entrance grave was noted here on the cliffs. Now only ruins of barrows here.

Tregeseal, St.Just [3891 3258]. There are 2 barrows to the NE of Tregeseal Circle on the way to the holed stones, one of which has a small chamber & may be the remains of an entrance grave.

Trendrine Hill nr Zennor [4787 3873]. There are 2 barrows on top of this hill, one of which may have been an entrance grave.

Try, near Newmill [4530 3606]. A former entrance grave with retaining wall, mostly demolished in 1963.

CONCLUSIONS

As the Quoits from the early Neolithic period went out of fashion, a new type of monument, the Entrance Grave or Chambered Tomb, began to be constructed. These are unique to West Penwith and the Isles of Scilly, and generally consist of a passage-like stone chamber roofed by a number of slabs, opening at one end to the outside, and surrounded by a kerb of large stone blocks. It still appears that bones and ashes from a number of individuals were deposited inside, similar to the Quoits that they replaced, so they may be thought of as communal burial places rather than monuments to single individuals.

It is the entrance orientations of the Entrance Graves that is most interesting. All of them seem to have significant orientations, either to midwinter solstice sunrise or sunset, or to special standstill positions of the moon. The midwinter was often associated with the dead, and some of the great tombs in other places dating from the same period, such as Newgrange in Ireland and Maes Howe on Orkney, were deliberately oriented to midwinter solstice sunrise or sunset. Bosiliack Barrow has an identical orientation to that of New-grange, and although on a much smaller scale, the intention may have been exactly the same. If Ian Cooke is right about the significance of the cup marks at Tregiffian Barrow, and they were carved to represent the moon's phases and to be seen by the dead inside the grave, then this would be additional evidence for the orientation of some of the tombs to lunar as well as solar events. It may well be that the dead were thought of as the 'guardians of the land' who watched over the fields and dwellings of the living, and who needed to be honoured and visited by the living, and to receive the energy of the sun and the moon.

BARROWS & CAIRNS

In addition to the sites recognised as Entrance Graves/Chambered Tombs, there are dozens of barrows scattered across the landscape of West Penwith. Vivien Russell in the *West Penwith Survey* lists over 250 barrows, barrow sites and field names indicating barrows once stood there. Many have been ploughed out, and some remain only as a hump in the ground, or denuded stones. The principal ones still worth visiting are listed on the map on p.34, and some of these are highlighted on the next 3 pages.

Chapel Carn Brea Long Cairn [3857 2799]. There were formerly 11 Barrows on the slopes and summit of the hill, but only 7 now remain, and most of these are in a ruinous condition. In addition to the Entrance Grave already listed *[p.28]*, there is a rare early Neolithic Long Cairn, which consists of a 11m (35½ft) linear stone mound built against a natural granite outcrop, situated on a false crest to the west of the summit. It is oriented NNW to SSE, and uses the natural rocky outcrop to extend its length by a further 26m (76ft). The rocky outcrop may have been perceived as being the dwelling place of spirits or deities, and the placing of the Cairn against the rocks may have denoted a sacred space which facilitated a direct connection between the spirits of the people (whose bones or ashes may have been buried within the cairn) and the spirits of the rocks.

St.Just - Sennen coastal barrows. The remains of a number of barrows can be seen running along the coast between St.Just and Sennen, all of which have views to the 'holy hilltop' of Chapel Carn Brea, to which they seem to be aligned. Running from St.Just westwards to Sennen along the coastal path, they are in order:
[1] Balowall Barrow/Carn Gluze [3555 3124], a barrow with entrance grave *[see p.28]*.
[2] Letcha Carn [3570 3025], a cairn with diameter of 8m (26ft) and a kerb surround of 4 remaining uprights.
[3] Boscregan Barrows: Carn Polpry (Carn Leskys) [3580 2983], one remaining cairn out of 3 original, consisting of a bank of earth and stone surrounded by a ring of (2) stones.
[4] Carn Creis: 2 cairns remain [4.1] Middle Cairn [3577 2969], originally 5.5m (18ft) in diameter, with outer & inner ring of stones & E-W oriented cist, east of centre. Kerb of 7 stones surrounds it. [4.2] Southern Cairn [3576 2966] *[photo right]* similar size with 6 stones in situ surrounding a natural granite boulder in centre of the barrow, perhaps mirroring the form of Chapel Carn Brea, visible to the east. Rich array of grave goods found, inc. 5 urns, blue faience beads, leaf-shaped arrowhead & perforated heart-shaped stone.

Carn Creis: southern cairn

St.Just - Sennen coastal barrows [cont].
[5] Escalls Cairn, Whitesands Bay [3623 2723], a small chambered cairn. Excavated by Borlase in 1879 who found the cairn had been built over a natural rock, surrounded by a double retaining wall. Burial cist contained flints & shells and a Middle Bronze Age urn.
[6] Mayon Cliff, Sennen [3482 2602]. Well preserved kerbed cairn, originally with cist *[photo right]*. Chapel Carn Brea only visible from site itself - in all other directions obscured by rising ground.

Mayon Cliff, Sennen

Tregeseal Barrows [3874 3259, 3887 3252, 3891 3258]
North of the stone circle there are a number of round barrows, which can be found by taking the path from the stone circle towards Carn Kenidjack and after about 100 yards bearing right (NE) along a smaller path towards the holed stones *[see p.21]*. The barrows will be visible ahead, and the path runs between two of the best preserved of them.
 The two best preserved barrows are 12.2m (40ft) & 14m (46ft) in diameter, and both about 1.5m (5ft) high. One of them [3887 3255] has part of its kerb remaining and may have held a cist (burial urn). The other [3891 3258] still has the remains of a stone chamber, which may have been an entrance grave [see p.30]. There is also another well-preserved barrow to the south at Hailglower Farm [3852 3210]. All these barrows were part of a funerary complex, and probably held the remains of the dead ancestors of the people who built the stone circle(s).

Nine Maidens Downs. A dug-out barrow encroaches on to the southern side of the circle *[see p.9]*, containing the remains of a central cist in which an urn and sherds of pottery were found. There is also a barrow with kerb stones further south at 4350 3496, kept uncovered by CASPN (Cornish Ancient Sites Protection Network). The remains of three more barrows lie to the north of the circle, one of which stands prominently on the summit of a ridge at 4327 3531 *[photo right]*, beside the path that leads to the stone circle from the Mên-an-Tol. This site was cleared of gorse and vegetation by CASPN in 2005, and one of

stones inside the barrow was discovered to have a seam of blue-grey crystal in a distinctive ^ shaped notch. This stone was presumably deliberately chosen because of its special appearance *[photo left]*.

Nine Maidens barrow where stone was found, with view towards Carn Gulva

Portheras Common [3914 3327]. At Potheras Common on a triangle of land east of B3306 & west of B3318 road. The barrow is 12.2m (40ft) in diameter & 0.8m (31in) high, and consists of a mound with surrounding kerbstones, with a central cist 1.2m (4ft) long & 0.6m (2ft) wide, roofed by a heavy capstone 1.8m (5¾ft) long. Excavated by W.C.Borlase, who found a cupped stone.

Close to the **Brane** entrance grave *[see p.27]* in the SW corner of the field, lies a probable long barrow [4019 2799] 6.1m (20ft) in diameter, 10m (12ft) wide & 2.2m (7ft) high. Where the Pendeen-Newbridge road meets the A3071 St.Just-Penzance road there is a line of 4 disc or platform barrows at **Botrea** (4023 3141, 4031 3133, 4032 3121 & 4033 3107). These climb a gentle hill rise from the valley floor below, aligned north-south, with each barrow coming into view from the preceeding one. The barrows vary in diameter from 16m (53ft) to 36m (118ft) and up to 1.5m (5ft) high. They have been excavated, and finds included urns, cremated ashes, and 2 arrowheads. As you approach the topmost barrow (4033 3107), the whole landscape of Sancreed Beacon, St. Michael's Mount and the Isles of Scilly come into view. This is clearly an Early Bronze Age sacred landscape, designed to be walked as a ceremonial path. To the west of the site there was a further 'arm' of 3 ring cairns or bowl barrows leading off from the main barrow at 4033 3107, perhaps a secondary sacred path.

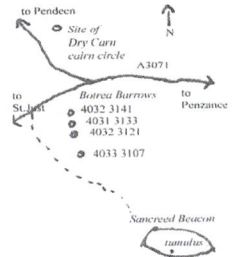

Further along this northern coast, there is a fine barrow on **Watch Croft hill** [4202 3571], close to the standing stone *[see p.17]* now unfortunately crowned with an OS trig pillar. Then at **Bosporthennis settlement** *[see p.37]* there are 3 barrows, all excavated by W.C.Borlase at 4448 3646 (circle of stones around a natural rock), 4453 3636 (another circle of stones around a natural rock) & 4407 3672 (mound with 2 retaining walls). Finally, there are 2 notable barrows on the top of **Trendrine Hill**. One of these [4787 3875] is a large cairn of stones 19m (62ft) in diamter & 2.6m (8½ft) high (with another trig pillar erected on it!), while the other [4787 3873] is a mound 14m (46ft) in diameter & 2m (6½ft) high, with a retaining kerb of very large stones incorporating the natural rock *[photo right]*. There is a Ley that runs along the top of the ridge from Zennor Quoit to this site *[see p.25]*, a track that rises up a slope

of land to the top of Trendrine Hill and the barrows, whereupon a great land and seacape opens up with a direct view to Trevalgan Hill, a breast-shaped mound, over which the midsummer sun rises from the sea - a truly wonderful piece of megalithic magic.

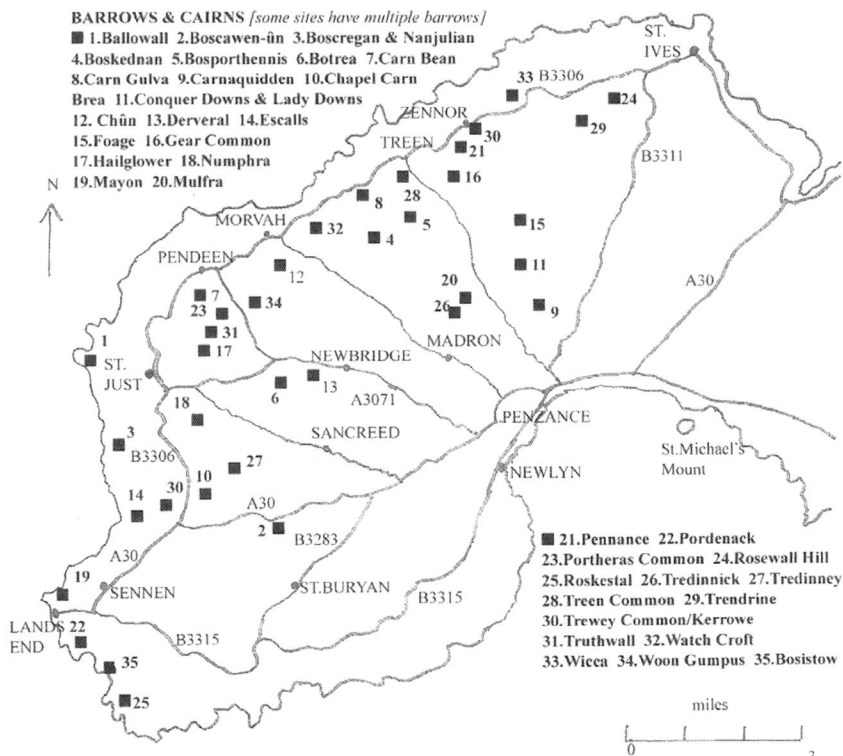

BARROWS & CAIRNS *[some sites have multiple barrows]*
■ 1.Ballowall 2.Boscawen-ûn 3.Boscregan & Nanjulian
4.Boskednan 5.Bosporthennis 6.Botrea 7.Carn Bean
8.Carn Gulva 9.Carnaquidden 10.Chapel Carn
Brea 11.Conquer Downs & Lady Downs
12. Chûn 13.Derval 14.Escalls
15.Foage 16.Gear Common
17.Hailglower 18.Numphra
19.Mayon 20.Mulfra

N

ST. IVES

33 B3306

ZENNOR

TREEN

■24
■29
■30
■21
B3311

MORVAH

■32
■4
■8
28
■5
■15

PENDEEN

12

■7
23
■34
■31
■17

NEWBRIDGE

20
26
■11
■9

MADRON

A30

ST. JUST

18
6
13
A3071

SANCREED

PENZANCE

St.Michael's Mount

NEWLYN

3
B3306
10
27

14
30
A30

2
B3283

19
SENNEN

ST.BURYAN

B3315

LANDS END
22
B3315
35

25

■ 21.Pennance 22.Pordenack
23.Portheras Common 24.Rosewall Hill
25.Roskestal 26.Tredinnick 27.Tredinney
28.Treen Common 29.Trendrine
30.Trewey Common/Kerrowe
31.Truthwall 32.Watch Croft
33.Wicca 34.Woon Gumpus 35.Bosistow

miles
0

CONCLUSIONS

Although it is generally assumed that barrows were burial mounds, that is not necessarily the case. The Cornish soil is very acidic, which means that, unless protected in urns or other containers, bones and other human remains are liable to be dissolved. Nevertheless, it is a fact that 45% of all Cornish barrows excavated by modern means have no traces of human burials whatsoever. Where there are remains, it appears that for these Bronze Age sites, multiple burials were the norm, not single individuals. What does this all mean? Current ideas are that these sites were not 'burial' places in the way that we think of them today: rather they were important symbolic symbols in the landscape. They were often aligned to significant landscape features, such as the coastal barrows to Chapel Carn Brea, the Boskednan barrows to Carn Gulva, and the Trendrine barrow to Trevalgan Hill. Furthermore, they seem to have been positioned as sightlines in the land. so that people following sacred paths to them would have features open up as they moved through the landscape. They have also been described as "powerful representations of the ancestral body in the landscape", that is, they were seen as the places of the collective stories and legends about the ancestors and their rôle in the oral history and myths of the tribe. West Penwith's Early Bronze Age communities seem to have had the ability and inclination to design and shape their immediate environment on a massive and complex scale, and to create barrows as the focii for their ceremonial practices and connection to the ancestors.

COURTYARD HOUSE SETTLEMENTS

During the Bronze Age, the people who built the megalithic monuments had generally lived in Round Houses, simple circular structures with walls of stone and thatched roofs. Remains of these 'hut circles' can be seen in various places in Cornwall. However, by the Iron Age (approx. 500 BCE to 500 CE), fashions began to change. Round Houses continued to be built, though they tended to be larger, and may have functioned as communal meeting places rather than individual dwellings. At the same time, from about the 1st century BCE in West Penwith (and only in West Penwith), people began to live in units that we now call Courtyard House Settlements. Typically these consisted of a number of individual buildings positioned around an unroofed courtyard. These buildings included dwelling houses, workshops, store-rooms and areas for animals. Each Courtyard House settlement would contain, on average, about 4 to 5 of these units, though there are larger ones (such as Chysauster) and also smaller ones, some of which contain only one unit. Some have fogous attached to the site [see p.39-44 for more details].

The remains of these Courtyard House settlements, in varying states of preservation, can be found all over West Penwith, and so far some 40 of these sites have been identified, with about half that number with extant remains. The map on p.38 shows the locations of 15 of those most worth visiting, and details of these are given over the next 3 pages.

Nanjulian [362 289]. This site is beautifully positioned overlooking the coast on the west side of Nanjulian valley near St.Just, and is reachable by a path down the valley leading across a stream. It consists of at least 3 courtyard houses, some round houses and a possible fogou *[see p.43]* with extensive terraced fields. There is a direct view to Chapel Carn Brea from the site, which was probably viewed as the place of the ancestors or Gods.

Carn Euny [402 288] Carn Euny Courtyard House Settlement can be found near the farmland of Brane, deep in the hidden heartland of West Penwith. From Sancreed take the signed turn. Small car park near site. Carn Euny is a fine example of a Courtyard House Settlement that was excavated in the 1960s. A timber-built settlement was started here in about 500BCE, which was later replaced by four interlocking courtyard houses, each containing a large court-yard, with adjoining spaces. Each house would have been roofed with thatch or turf over a timber framework, and the whole 'village' would have been a secure and self-contained unit. Magnificent fogou remains *[see p.40]*. Some tin streaming may have taken place, along with weaving and corn-grinding: pottery and various types of stone tools that were found on the site are indicative of this. The inhabitants worked the surrounding fields, and there is no evidence of any tribal fighting here: the settlement was abandoned peacefully in about the 5th century CE.

Trewern [428 322] near Newbridge. 1 Courtyard House and remains of fields and enclosures, immediately behind Higher Trewern Farmhouse. The site may have contained a fogou. Trewern Round lies 553m (600 yds) to the SE, with Trewern standing stone nearby *[see p.16]*.

Goldherring [415 324] near Sancreed. A single courtyard house inside an earlier Round, surrounded by terraced fields - also one Round House. Excavated 1958-1962. On Boscawen-ûn Circle Ley [5] *(see p.7)* & Ley from Drift menhirs - Goldherring Courtyard House settlement - Brane entrance grave - Missing stone at Chapel Carn Brea 3814 2799.

Croftoe [403 348] near Morvah. 4 Courtyard houses, 2 forming a semi-detached unit. Part of one house excavated in 1922. In low-lying position close to head of stream.

Trevean [413 357] near Morvah. 3 Courtyard houses, recently cleared by National Trust. Large contemporary terraced fields & possible fogou that was destroyed in 1913*[see p.43]*.

Bosullow Trehyllis [409 342] at base of Chûn Hill. 4, possibly 5, Courtyard houses, and at least 13 round houses, surrounded by well-preserved paddocks and garden plots. Possible small above-ground fogou with creep passage at edge of one of the Courtyard Houses*[see p.43]*. Unexcavated and in extremely good condition, but access limited by landowner. Ley found by John Michell: Bosullow Trehyllys - Mên-an-Tol - Boundary stones - Round field 4642 3659 - Tumulus 4748 3707.

Bosigran East [428 370] West [423 371]. Two settlements in fields north of B3306 near coast, with good views south to Carn Gulva. Bosigran East has 1 Courtyard House and possible remains of 2 more, one of which, a stone mound, may contain remains of a fogou. Nearby is a well-preserved Round. Bosigran West has 3, possibly 4 Courtyard Houses (2 of which are well preserved), and a Round House, scattered in fields that may be part of the original field system. Bosigran Cliff Castle is 460m (500yds) to the W.

Porthmeor [434 371]. On Porthmeor Farm, on B3306 road. Standing stone *[see p.17]* on north side of road, settlement on south side. An extensive settlement, with 3 Courtyard Houses, 8 Round Houses, paved courts and roadways inside a secondary oval Round. Outside, there are 3 Round Houses and a further Courtyard House, adjoined by an above-ground fogou *[see p.43]*. Excavated 1933-35.

Treen [437 372]. Not far fron the Treen Entrance Graves *[see p.29]*. Site consists of 4 Courtyard Houses, 2 connected to form a semi-detached unit, within well-preserved paddocks and terraces, still retaining gateways. All houses have entrances untypically facing west (most Courtyard Houses face in an easterly direction).

Bosporthennis [438 361]. (pronounced *Bosprennis*) Remote site, approachable from lane leading through Bosporthennis Farm from Gurnards Head-Newmill road. At least 3 Court-yard Houses, possibly as many as 5, in a widely scattered settlement in the lee of Hannibal's Carn. Stands within contemporary field system, but most distinctive feature is a Beehive Hut [4379 3596], *[photo right]*, consisting of a round corbelled chamber 4m (13ft) in diameter, connected to a rectangular room 3.4m (13ft) x 2.1m (7ft) by a low but massive doorway. The Beehive Hut is almost identical to the one at Carn Euny settlement that leads off the fogou *[see p.40]*, with a similar recess inside. There have been some suggestions that the rectangular room is part of the remains of an above-ground fogou, but this seems unlikely.

Interior of Beehive Hut

Try Farm [461 355] near Newmill. 2, perhaps 3, Courtyard Houses above Try Farm, just south of Try round, near Try menhir *[see p.17 & 18]*. One House is widely surrounded by embanked enclosure with inturned entrance.
Cranken [461 334] near Newmill. 2 Courtyard Houses in large terraced field system containing at least 3 Round Houses. To the west of Courtyard Houses is a Round.

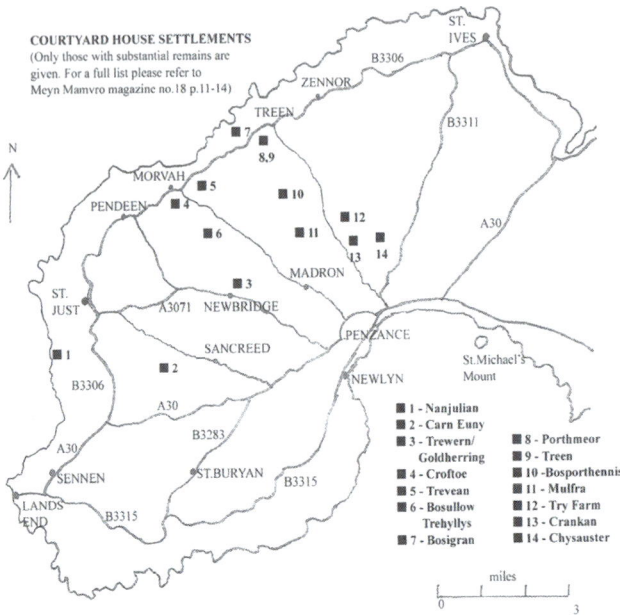

N

ST. IVES
B3306
ZENNOR
TREEN
7
8,9
MORVAH
5
10
PENDEEN
4
12
6
11
13 14
MADRON
3
ST. JUST
A3071 NEWBRIDGE
SANCREED
PENZANCE
St.Michael's Mount
NEWLYN
B3306
A30
A3283
A30
SENNEN
ST.BURYAN B3315
LANDS END B3315

B3306
B3311
A30

1 - Nanjulian
2 - Carn Euny
3 - Trewern/Goldherring
4 - Croftoe
5 - Trevean
6 - Bosullow Trehyllys
7 - Bosigran
8 - Porthmeor
9 - Treen
10 - Bosporthennis
11 - Mulfra
12 - Try Farm
13 - Crankan
14 - Chysauster

miles
0   3

Mulfra [453 349]. Near Newmill at southern foot of Mulfra Hill. An extensive site with 3 fine Courtyard Houses on one side of track and others to north of these. Site is cleared and managed by CASPN regularly. 3 Leys go through this site: [1] Tregeseal Circle Ley [1] *(see p.8)* [2] Mên-an-Tol- Mulfra courtyard house settlement - Try menhir - Chysauster courtyard house settlement - Castle-an-Dinas 485 350. [3] Boswartha Carn 427 332 - Enclosure 4340 3352 - Carfury menhir - Mulfra courtyard house settlement - Try Courtyard House settlement.

Bodrifty [445 354]. Just north of Mulfra is a settlement of 8 Round Houses lying within a low oval and stone wall. 1951-5 excavations revealed drains, hearths & pottery sherds. Owners of Bodrifty Farm nearby have built a full scale reconstruction of a House *[photo right]*.

Chykembro [447 371]. On hillside behind Pennance Farm, near Zennor. 1 Courtyard House, 4-5 Round Houses & small enclosure. Site recently cleared by National Trust.

Chysauster [472 350]. The most extensive and well preserved Courtyard House Settlement in West Penwith. Open to public [admission charge]. 11, probably 12, courtyard houses, 8 of them in pairs alongside village street., with attached garden plots. Large field system alongside, containing Round Houses (partially destroyed in 1984). Ruinous fogou to south of main village (now fenced off- *see p.43*). Site excavated with finds of pottery & cream-coloured quartz pebbles. In 2003 a tiny (2cm) copper alloy spoon was discovered, which may have been used for eating shellfish. Fine site.

Fogous are always found as part of Courtyard House settlements, and date from the same Celtic Iron Age period (500 BCE-500CE approx), but, for example in the case of Carn Euny, we know that the fogou was there *before* the Courtuard Houses were built around it. Fogous seem to have been the sacred centres of the Courtyard House villages, and the predominant view nowadays are that they were used not for refuge or storage but for ceremony and ritual. They are (usually) curved underground passageways, with a narrow side passage known as a 'creep' sloping towards the surface, which was probably the original entrance. Both ends of the fogou may have originally been sealed, and entering them feels like going into the Underworld: "a dank, dark cave of pulsating energies where unexpected things can occur". People often seem to have psychic or altered state of consciousness experiences in them. One woman artist has spoken of Boleigh fogou being a gateway to the unconscious, which helped her reach within herself for levels of dream and vision which enriched and added meaning to her life and pictures. Jo May, who formerly ran a Healing Centre where Boleigh fogou lies, has also talked about fogous being used for spiritual practices involving death and rebirth, vision quests, healing and inner guidance.

Fogous seem to reflect back to us what is happening in our own lives: at times they can feel very peaceful, almost soporific. One visitor to Carn Euny fogou who was sketching there one day felt she was being watched. Glancing over her shoulder she saw a mother and child looking at her through a window of one of the ancient houses that no longer exists! She had a feeling of great peace and love from her vision. Another local woman heard strange voices in the chamber, some whispering, some talking excitedly, some murmuring in her ear. It was as if the spirits of the people who lived there were still hovering around. At other times fogous may seem uninviting or overwhelming. Someone who went for the first time to Boleigh fogou found the entrance blocked by two large megalithic slabs. Thinking this was normal, she went away, only to find out later that there were no entrance slabs there within recorded memory (though there may have been originally). It was as if she were not yet ready to enter the fogou. Truly, fogous are very special spiritual places: approach them with reverence for they are sacred passageways into the living earth herself.

CARN EUNY [4024 2885]

This well-preserved fogou is part of Carn Euny Courtyard House settlement *[see p.36]*. It consists of a roofed underground tunnel 20m (66ft) in length and over 1.8m (6ft) high. Both ends are now open, though originally both were sealed, and the only way into the fogou would have been by means of a tiny creep passage at the south end, which would only have been accessible by crawling down it. The fogou originally had a paved floor with drainage channels. To the north of the fogou and attached to it is a Beehive Hut, a corbelled chamber 4.6m (15ft) in diameter and 2.4m (8ft) high. It is completely below ground level, but there is some doubt as to whether it would originally have been roofed or not. Today an artificial roof that was subsequently grassed over has been placed on it.

The fogou had three successive phases of development. The **first** phase (around the 5th century BCE) was the construction of the corbelled Beehive Hut, which was deliberately oriented to the SE to face the first rays of the rising sun at the Midwinter solstice. Opposite the entrance on the back wall is a recess, which may have been designed as a kind of 'altar' to catch the rising sunlight. The **second** phase saw the contruction of the fogou in about 300-50BCE, which was attached to the Beehive Hut, with an entance in its northerly wall. The northerly end of the fogou faces NE, the direction of the Midsummer solstice, but it is likely that both north and south ends of the fogou were sealed at this time, and entry could only be made

Development of fogou

by the small creep passage at the southern end. The fogou originally had a paved floor with drainage channels. Finally, by the time of the **third** phase (by 1st century CE) the earlier timber and stone dwellings on the site had been replaced by permanent courtyard houses, and one was built that incorporated both fogou and beehive hut, with an entrance made from the house directly into the NE end of the fogou. The house may thus have served as some kind of ante-chamber or preparation room for entering the fogou, perhaps used on occasions of ritual and ceremony, in place of the creep passage.

The site was eventually abandoned and deliberately filled in with earth. It was rediscovered in the 1860s, when some pottery fragments and ashes were found, and was fully excavated in the 1960s. It is freely open at all times for visitors.

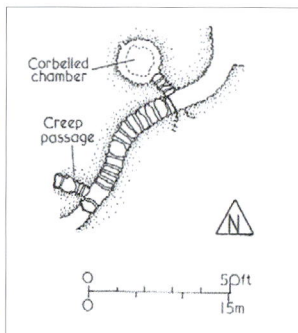

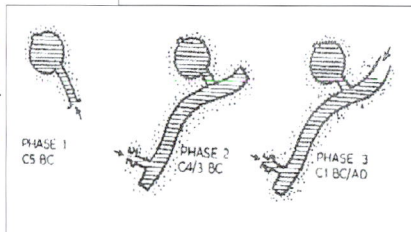

BOLEIGH [4370 2520]

This site lies in the grounds of Rosmerryn House near Lamorna, about ¼mile east of the Merry Maidens stone circle. Permission to visit should be obtained, preferably by phone (01736-810530). The fogou now stands alone in the grounds of the House, but was formerly contained within an earthwork (measuring 43m (140ft) x 24m (80ft)), and was undoubtedly part of a Courtyard House settlement, where Rosmerryn House now stands. The fogou itself is beautifully preserved with a main chamber 10.9m (36ft) long and 1.8m (6ft) high, which is entered from the SW but once again is oriented to the NE, the direction of the midsummer solstice sunrise.

Once again, like Carn Euny, the fogou may have been blocked at both ends, with entry from above being through the small creep passage on the west side of the chamber, which is now blocked at its southern end. Alternatively, the creep passage may only have been accessible from inside the fogou itself - it is not really known for certain. If it were the only entry from outside, it would have involved dropping into the creep, and then having to turn sharp right and crawl on hands and knees into the main chamber, which would have been a powerful initiatory experience. However, others have suggested that the creep passage was designed as an inner chamber, accessible only from the fogou, with space enough only comfortably for one person, which may have served as a meditation space, or even perhaps a birthing chamber.

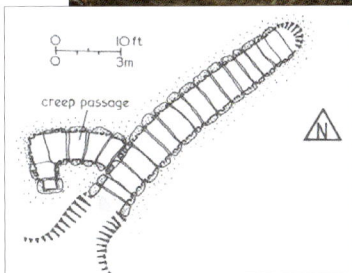

It has been suggested that there is an indistinct carving on the left hand upright stone of the present-day SW entrance *[drawing right]*. This has been seen as an upper part of a figure, carrying a stave or spear in one hand and a lozenge or possibly serpent's head in the other. This has been variously interpreted as a symbol of a fertility cult to ensure a successful harvest (Evelyn Clarke in *Cornish Fogous*); a Celtic hooded godlet - genii cucullati - found elsewhere in Gaul (Craig Weatherhill); a Celtic god of healing, Clew an Nemed, found elsewhere in Brittany (Jo May in *Living with a Fogou* Meyn Mamvro no.3); or a Cernunumnos figure - the Celtic horned god with his serpent and remains of a horn. It has to be said that the 'carving' is now virtually impossible to see, so its provenance and veracity must remain a mystery.

Also mysterious at this site is the presence of anomalous light phenonema, seen by Jo May and others, and described as "hundreds of tiny pricks of light, like stars, moving gently". This 'star soup' may be a manifestation of a little-understood 'earth lights' phenonema produced by some kind of electromagnetic energy, not understood by conventional science, but also seen at other sites, for example Chûn Quoit *[see p.24]*.

41

PENDEEN [3837 3553]

This is a superb fogou in a rather mundane location - at the back of a farmyard through a muddy cow byre. At Portheras Cross near Pendeen take the road leading down to the lighthouse, and about ¼mile before the end, take the right turn to Manor Farm, where there is informal parking on the grass verge, and ask permission at the Farm.

The fogou opens from the side of an ancient stone hedge and descends steeply underground, then levels and turns sharply left. The total length of this angled passage is 17.2m (56½ft), and after it bends left, the orientation of the passage is in a NW direction, which is the direction of the midsummer solstice sunset. At the angle of the passage there is a quartz stone built into the wall, perhaps placed deliberately to indicate the sacred direction. At this point, to the right in a NE direction, there is a closed chamber (which may have been the original entrance 'creep') which was cut from the main clay with no supporting stonework. The entrance to this rab-cut chamber is just 0.6m (2ft) wide and 0.5m (1½ft) high, and it leads into the chamber 7.3m (24ft) long, 1.5m (5ft) wide & 1.2m (4ft) high. Again, like the extant creeps in the other fogous, this is a belly-crawling experience, not for those with claustrophobia!

There is a legend associated with the fogou of a woman in white who appears with a red rose in her mouth at the entrance on Christmas morning. She comes from Ireland, and portends death to anyone who sees her. This may be a folk memory of winter solstice rituals performed at the fogou, in connection with the Goddess and spirits of the dead ancestors (who indeed may originally have come from Ireland to Cornwall in Celtic times).

LOWER BOSCASWELL [3767 3484]

About ½mile west of Pendeen fogou lie the remains of Lower Boscaswell fogou. This can be reached by taking the road leading down to the coast from Boscaswell Stores, parking at the bottom, and taking the track on the right that leads to a field on the left. Only the entrance to the chamber still exists, with the remnants of a small creep passage, but the orientation of this chamber, like the chamber of Pendeen fogou, is to the NW, the midsummer solstice sunset *[photo right]*. The remainder of the chamber, which originally would have been at least 5.2m (17ft) long has since been destroyed, so that the site now more resembles an entrance grave than a fogou. Nevertheless it is interesting to see that both Pendeen and Boscaswell could have been 'sunset' fogous.

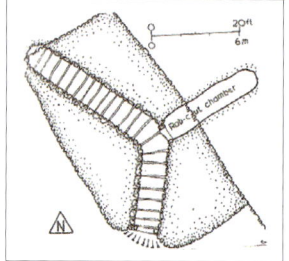

42

OTHER FOGOUS (Partial remains)

Porthmeor [4341 3703]. On Porthmeor Farm (private) and now quite overgrown. Like Carn Euny, Porthmeor fogou lies at the edge of a Courtyard House settlement *[see p.37]*. Like other fogous it had a curved passage (13m (43ft long & 1.7m (5½ft) high), but unlike others it appears to have been above ground, and roofed by corbelling and lintels, though it is now roofless. Like most of the other fogous, its northerly passage seems to be oriented NE, the direction of the midsummer solstice sunrise.

Chysauster [4720 3483]. This underground fogou, which stands on the edge of Chysauster Courtyard House settlement *[see p.38]*, has only 2 roofing lintels over a small entrance remaining, although it was originally about 15m (50ft) long, with corbelled walls. It was excavated in the 19th century by W.C.Borlase but is now fenced off and not accessible *[photo right]*.

DESTROYED SITES

Higher Bodinar [4150 3230]. Situated near Sancreed, and known as The Giants Holt, it existed in a ruined form until the early years of the 20th century, but now destroyed.

Castallack [app.4515 2531]. Situated near Paul, this probable fogou passageway was discovered in 1866 and plotted and drawn by J.T.Blight at the time, but now destroyed.

POSSIBLE SITES

In his book *Mother and Sun: the Cornish fogou,* Ian Cooke lists a possible additional 18 sites in West Penwith and 10 more outside, taken from earlier descriptions of sites and field names. In West Penwith these include: Trevean at Morvah [app.4122 3578], Bosigran near Zennor [app.4281 3694], Bosullow near Chûn [4097 3420], and Nanjulian between St.Just & Sennen [3614 2891]. For sites outside West Penwith see next page for full details.

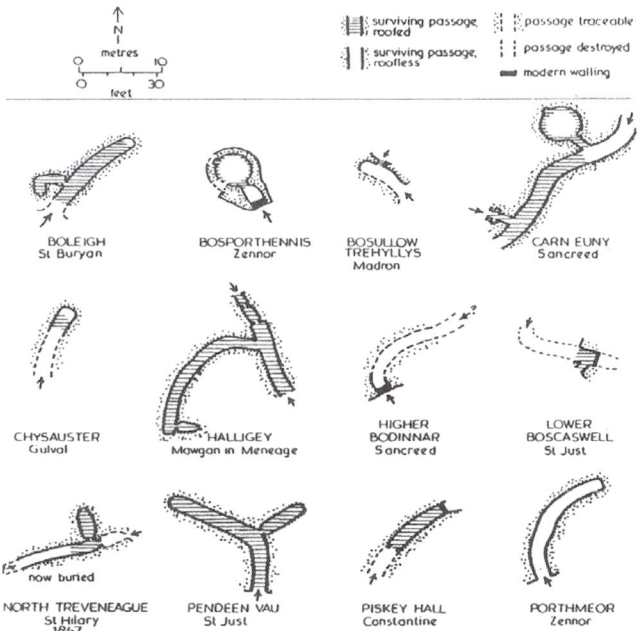

Orientation of fogous in west Cornwall

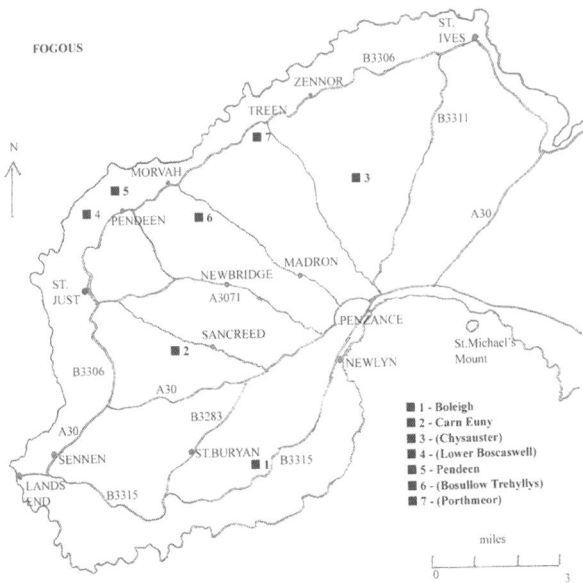

FOGOUS

ST. IVES
B3306
ZENNOR
TREEN
B3311
MORVAH ■7
■5 ■3
■4 PENDEEN ■6
A30
MADRON
NEWBRIDGE
ST. A3071
JUST
PENZANCE
SANCREED St.Michael's
■2 Mount
B3306 NEWLYN
A30
B3283
A30
SENNEN ST.BURYAN
LANDS ■1 B3315
END B3315

1 - Boleigh
2 - Carn Euny
3 - (Chysauster)
4 - (Lower Boscaswell)
5 - Pendeen
6 - (Bosullow Trehyllys)
7 - (Porthmeor)

miles
0   3

OTHER SITES All fogous are in the west of Cornwall, and most in West Penwith: no fogou sites have been positively identified outside this area. The principal other sites outside of West Penwith are: Halligye on the Trelowarren Estate [7132 2395], a large well-preserved fogou; and Piskey Hall at Trewardreva [7280 3003], which has a short passage with no creep. In addition a large fogou was explored and drawn by J.T.Blight in 1867 at Treveneague near St. Hilary [app.5484 3315], but is now lost; and a fogou at Boden on the Lizard [7685 2406] has recently been partially excavated.

CONCLUSIONS

Fogous continue to be something of an enigma. Suggestions have been made that they were places of refuge, but with only one entrance/exit this seems unlikely. Or that they were storage chambers for food, but they would have been too damp to have been very successful. A ritual or ceremonial use seems much more likely. Ian Cooke discovered that all the extant sites have the northern end of their passages aligned to the rising Midsummer sun, except for the north coast ones, Pendeen and Boscaswell, and they face the setting Midsummer sun. So it would seem likely that they had a ceremonial function relating to the solar cycle. Recently, it has been pointed out that tin loads in West Penwith run in a NE-SW direction, and many fogous are near to these loads, so perhaps it also had to do with honouring or propitiating the Earth Goddess into whose body they had dug.

Other suggestions have been that fogous were continuing into the Iron Age the sacred function of barrows in the Bronze Age, and before that the use of caves by the Paleolithic and Mesolithic peoples. They may have been important places where individuals went at 'turning points' in their existence; for example, conception, birth, menstruation, initiation, pair bonding, sickness and death. Or they may have been places where the initiates or shamans of the tribe would go to contact the spirit world through prolonged states of trance where visions and dreams could be more easily experienced. The fact that people today continue to have visionary experiences in them might confirm this. Most fogous have a very high interior radiation, and it has been suggested that this, together with perhaps meditation, chanting and drumming and the ingestion of psychotropic substances, might lead to altered states of consciousness. They might also have been symbolic ritual passages where ceremonies would have been performed for the ancestors, or to connect with the revitalising energies of the reborn Sun God/dess. Whatever their precise function, it does seem that they were powerful spiritual and psychic places, and continue so today.

44

HILL FORTS & CLIFF CASTLES

Hill Forts and Cliff Castles are both the product of the Celtic Iron Age period (though Hill Forts often began to be constructed in the late Bronze Age). Both are somewhat enigmatic: the terminology 'forts' and 'castles' implies a defensive function, though it is far from certain that this was their only or main purpose. They can be found throughout Cornwall, and the next few pages list some of the main ones in West Penwith.

HILL FORTS

Hill Forts are nearly always (though not exclusively) on the top of hills, with wide panoramic views of the surrounding land. They are round or oval in plan, and usually have earth ramparts of one or two lines. There is evidence of Round Houses built within, but whether these were permanently or seasonally occupied is not known. It may well be that Hill Forts were kept for protection of the people in times of conflict, and were otherwise resorted to on special occasions, such as communial gatherings for trade and festivities.

St.Michael's Mount [515 299]. This iconic place (reached by a causeway at low tide and a boat at high) was in the Neolithic period joined to the mainland until rising sea levels separated it in about 2500 BCE. Its Cornish name *Carriek Loos y'n Coos* ('grey rock in the wood') recalls that time, and remnants of an ancient forest have been found in Mounts Bay. By the Iron Age, it was operating as a trading port, and the site of round houses has been found on its eastern side. Four great energy lines, named Michael & Mary and Apollo & Athena meet at the edge of this island.

Lescudjack [475 310]. The remains of this hill fort lie beside Castle Road, Penzance and, although the gardens of a housing estate intrude into half the area, the remainderof the fort has recently been excavated and restored. It was originally oval in shape and was the largest of West Penwith's hill forts, measuring 152m (500ft) by 122m (400ft).

Faughan Round [452 282]. The remains of a hill fort 122m (400ft) in diameter, with extensive views over Mounts Bay. Remains of two concentric ramparts, some of which has been ploughed out. Two upright stones remain, which were the gateposts of the inner entrance *[photo right]*.

Lesingey Round [453 304]. Reached by a lane leading off the A3071 Penzance-St.Just road. The smallest of the hill forts 79m (260ft) in diameter. Single earth rampart, reaching height of 3.7m (12ft) above ditch. Now wooded over whole Round.

Faughan Round

Bartinney [395 293]   Bartinney and Chapel Carn Brea are the two prominent hills seen throughout West Penwith. Bartinney is 224m (734ft) high and is crowned with a circular earthwork 75m (246ft) across, in the centre of which are the remains of three ring cairns, (with traces of other cairns around), probably dating from an earlier period. This may have been a late Neolithic or Bronze Age sacred enclosure of some kind, which was developed by the Iron Age people into an (unfinished) hill fort.

Caer Bran [408 290].   On this neighbouring 190m (624ft) high hill is a similar sacred enclosure with three ring cairns from the Bronze Age that was developed in the Iron Age into a hill fort 131m (430ft) in diameter, with two concentric ramparts. Fine views.

Chûn Castle [405 339] On this 215m (706ft) hill lies the remains of Chûn Castle, an Iron Age hill fort, built during the 3rd century BCE. Although robbed of stone in the 19thC, much of the Castle with its thick walls remains. It is 85m (280ft) in diameter and consists of 2 concentric granite walls and ditches around an inner courtyard, which contained Iron Age huts. In the 6th century CE it was extensively remodelled with the building of 15-16 houses. About ¼mile to the west lies Chûn Quoit *[see p.24].*

Carn Gulva [426 364]. A 210m (682ft) high rocky outcrop on the northern Penwith moors. Accessible by pathways from the B3306 north coast road, and also from Nine Maidens Downs to the south. It was originally a Neolithic tor enclosure (sacred hilltop) that continued into use in later periods. A site where hut circles were constructed has been identified on a flat area north of the summit.

Castle-an-Dinas [485 350].   The path to the top of this hill fort runs beside a large quarry. At 133m (435ft) in diameter, it originally had 2 massive concentric walls, an earth and stone rampart, and an outer rampart, though much of this is now in ruins, with a folly (Roger's Tower) built in 1798 from much of the stone. In the centre of the fort are 3 circular structures, which may have been ring cairns, similar to Bartinney & Caer Bran.

Trencrom Hill [518 362]. Accessible from the A3074 at Lelant, this is a beautiful 160m (520ft) hill with views northwards to St.Ives Island (and the Hayle estuary), and southwardsto St.Michael's Mount (an energy line crosses all three sites). First occupied during the Neolithic and Bronze Age, it was used again as an Iron Age hill fort, when a pear-shaped enclosure 137m (450ft) x 91m (300ft) was constructed. Inside there are the remains of 3 earlier ring cairns + 6 Round House platforms. Beersheba standing stone in field N of site *[p.18].*

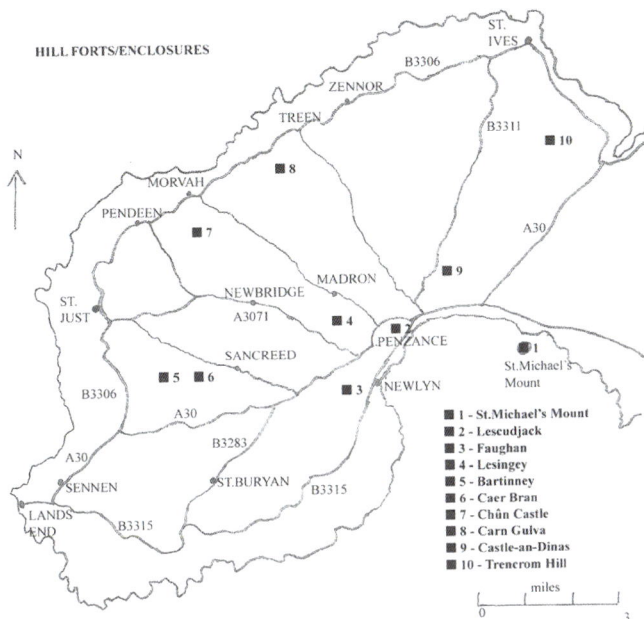

Map legend:
- 1 - St.Michael's Mount
- 2 - Lescudjack
- 3 - Faughan
- 4 - Lesingey
- 5 - Bartinney
- 6 - Caer Bran
- 7 - Chûn Castle
- 8 - Carn Gulva
- 9 - Castle-an-Dinas
- 10 - Trencrom Hill

ROUNDS

Rounds are curious Iron Age structures that are generally on lower-lying land than Hill Forts (though Faughan is both a Hill Fort and a Round), and in two cases (Goldherring & Porthmeor) the Round enclosed Courtyard Houses. Rounds may have been used for animal pounds, or had a land use. Examples include Caergwidden Round, nr Newbridge [415 310], Castallack Round [448 254] & Kerris Round [445 272] near Paul, Trevean Round nr Morvah [413 353] & Trewern Round nr Newbridge [433 320].

CLIFF CASTLES

Cliff Castles date from the same Iron Age period as Hill Forts. and may also have been used intermittently as defensive places. They are positioned on headlands, where they utilise the rocky seaward side as a natural barrier, and fortify the narrow neck of land with defensive banks and ditches. However, it has also been suggested that they may have been envisioned as sacred places, at a liminal spot between land and sea. There are 33 of them throughout Cornwall, and 8 of the best in West Penwith are listed below.

Treryn Dinas [397 231]. Near Porthcurno, this spectacular cliff castle incorporates the famous natural feature of the Logan Rock. The cliff castle itself has no less than four lines of defences, with ramparts and ditches, and at the furthest seaward line, remains of two hut circles. The presence of the Logan Rock (rocking stone) may have been seen as a magical feature to the cliff castle builders.

Carn Les Boel [357 233]. This Cliff Castle stands on a headland near Lands End, on the southern side of Nanjisal Bay. The Cliff Castle is protected by two earth and stone ramparts, and on the central ridge of the headland are two large stones, one upright and one fallen, which may have been the jamstones of the entrance. According to Hamish Miller & Paul Broadhust, the great energy line known as the Michael Line comes onto (or leaves) the coast at this point - "the broad band of energy converged to a point at a great slab of horizonal granite, disappeared into the ground, and then re-appeared".

Maen Castle [348 258]. This site *[right]* stands between Sennen & Lands End, and excavations in 1939 & 1948 showed it to have been built before 300 BCE, making it the probable earliest Cliff Castle. The small rocky headland was defended by a stone wall, ditch and bank. Narrow gateway with well preserved stones.

Cape Cornwall [353 318]. This distinctive prominatory outside St.Just (thought in the Middle Ages to be the Lands End itself) had 3 ramparts and ditches, which were destroyed in the late 19thC.
Kenidjack Castle [356 326]. The neighbouring headland of Kenidjack was a Cliff Castle with an outer ditch and 3 ramparts, with traces of hut circles. The site was the source of Neolithic axes, and in the Bronze Age tin was probably mined here and traded.

Bosigran Castle [417 369]. A single wall 1.5m (5ft) high encloses this dramatically positioned Cliff Castle. Nearby are remains of Courtyard House settlements *[see p.37],* all on the northward side of Carn Gulva.

Gurnards Head [433 385]. Also known as Treen Dinas, this Cliff Castle has two ramparts & three ditches across a narrow neck of headland. A number of hut circles were found on the headland behind the defences, in 2 groups 46m (50 yds) & 173m (190 yds) north of the inner rampart.

Bosigran from Carn Gulva

St. Ives Island [520 411]. The former name of this headland Pendinas ('head of the fort') or Dinas Ia ('fort of St,Ia) gives an indication that this prominatory was once a Cliff Castle, now crowned by the remains of a chapel. This narrow neck of land from St.Ives to St. Michaels Mount would in the Iron Age & early Christian period be the easiset way to cross from Ireland & Wales to Brittany, and is now a footpath known as the St.Michaels Way, running through Trencrom Hill *[p.46*

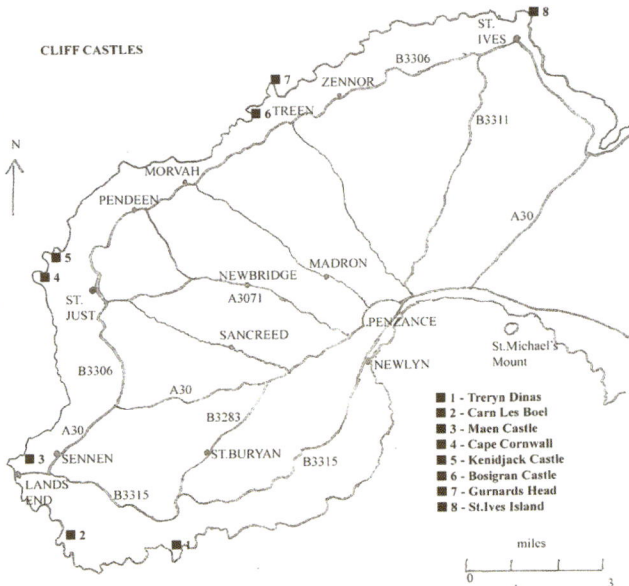

CLIFF CASTLES

1 - Treryn Dinas
2 - Carn Les Boel
3 - Maen Castle
4 - Cape Cornwall
5 - Kenidjack Castle
6 - Bosigran Castle
7 - Gurnards Head
8 - St.Ives Island

miles

Water is the essence of life itself, and the holy wells of West Penwith contain the quintessence of that sacred water. Half-hidden at the end of secret pathways, stumbled upon near old streams, nestling at the bottom of remote valleys far from the roads and cottages of modern-day Penwith, these ancient places of healing and contemplation are refuges from the strains and pressures of 20th century 'civilisation'. They link us back to a more mysterious, more spiritual past, back to the early days of the Celtic saints, and back even before then; for surely they were pagan places of veneration long before they became Christianised, a time when humankind lived in mutual harmony with the spirit of the Earth Mother. At these natural springs, ancient peoples would have learnt much holy well lore, secrets of healing and divination, cures and visions from the Earth herself. The memory of the efficacy of these special places endured over the centuries, and the wells continued to be visited by custom right up until the middle of the 20th century.

And so they continue to be visited, perhaps more now than ever. Some over the years have been destroyed or become desecrated, but many still remain, a testimony to the continuing power and attraction of these places of peace. Here we can sit in contemplation, undisturbed by the throng of too many people; here we can touch the ancient moss-covered stones surrounding the wells and connect with a time long past; here we can reach down and scoop up some of the cold clear waters for sipping or splashing on our hurts. Sometimes we will find flowers left as an offering to the spirits of the well, or rags left in a tree nearby,following an age-old custom. Here we can still the pounding of our busy brains, here we can cure the sicknesses within ourselves, here we can learn to respect and love the earth anew. Here we can see the afternoon sun or the rising moon shining their lights into the sacred shrines themselves, as we sit quietly meditating, accompanied perhaps only by the gentle dryads, the spirits of the well itself, hovering peacefully around the cool clear waters. Here we can attune ourselves to the harmony of the waters of the wells, wells that are still alive today with power to heal or give insights into the past, present and future, if only we care for them as they were cared for all those hundreds and thousands of years ago.

49

MADRON WELL & BAPTISTRY

[4465 3280]. Signposted down a green lane to the north of Madron village. Follow the path from the car parking area to the 'Cloutie Trees' (trees festooned with coloured rags and pieces of cloth). Here there is a small stone marker sign set into the ground, pointing right to the Baptistry and left to the Well. (Note that the area below the Cloutie Tree is not the actual well). The well lies about ¼ mile into the boggy area and is identifiable by a stone enclosure of gran-

Madron Baptistry (Well-Chapel)

ite slabs, which are submerged below the water in particularly wet conditions. This stone surround was rebuilt in the early 1980s from stones found in the area, so it may not be exactly how the pre-Christian well originally looked. The Baptistry is a small roofless rectangular building, with an altar stone at the eastern end and a well with running water in the SW corner. This water was originally channeled here from the source of the Holy Well itself although nowadays it also contains run-off water from the surrounding fields. The present building dates from about the 12th century, though there was probably a simple building here from Celtic times onwards.

The earliest reference to this site was in 1640, when it was recorded that the "cripple John Trelill" came here and bathed once a week for three weeks in May. He then slept on a mound nearby called St.Maddern's Bed (the location of which is now not known) and was cured. From then onwards, the site was much visited and venerated. It is sometimes not clear as to whether it is the Holy Well or this Baptistry Well that is being visited, but children were certainly brought to one or other, stripped naked and plunged three times through the water widdershins (against the sun, or anti-clockwise) to restore their health. In the 19th Century, an old dame An Kitty used to attend the Baptistry (or well) in the Springtime to instruct 'the gentry' (who were then beginning to visit sites such as these) on the 'correct rituals' to perform at the well, which unfortunately are not recorded.

ALSIA [3935 2512]. This beautiful but little-known well is approachable from the St.Buryan to Sennen minor road at a bend in the road just above Alsia Mill. A permissive path goes to the site, which nestles down the bottom of a steeply-sloping field, and is enclosed by iron railings and a gate. A very peaceful place.

There is no known saints' attribution to this well, but it was certainly considered to be a powerful healing well. On the first three Wednesdays in May weak and rickety children would be brought to the well, and it was also used for prophecy by young women who would drop pebbles or pins into its waters to see how many years their relationships would last, the number of bubbles rising indicating the number of years.

SANCREED [Chapel Downs] [4180 2935]

Approachable either from a path opposite Sancreed Church by a telephone box, or by one opposite Sancreed Beacon. It lies in a grove of conifers, holly and shrubs, which were probably planted when the well was rediscovered by Rev. Reginald Basset Rogers in 1879. Steps lead steeply down into the well, with a womb-like chamber, aglow with moss-green phosporesence: a truly numinous place. Above the well are the remains of a Celtic Chapel, and next to this a modern cross, erected in 1910.

There are no known cures associated with this well, but there are some anomalous experiences reported. In his book *Places of Power* Paul Devereux comments: "The prime energy effect of the place is the sense of calm it engenders. Peace. Repose. I have actually seen every person in a group of 15 people enter a deep, languid state here, or fall completely asleep! It is a place to sleep; to have the Dream of Earth. The waters at Sancreed have given me (with their permission) the highest radiation counts I have obtained anywhere in Cornwall, registering here nearly 200% overall above background. I suspect that at particular wells or springs, radiation languor was one of the factors used to help induce trance-like states conducive to visionary and divinatory work".

CHAPEL EUNY [3999 2990].

To the west of Carn Euny courtyard house settlement, lying either side of an ancient trackway, are these twin holy wells. At the larger, and better-known, well seven steps lead down to the water, which flows away under a large lintel as the infant Lamorna stream. The opening of the well is surrounded by worked stones from the former chapel of St.Uny, which stood a few paces NE.

The water was considered extremely potent for all manner of ills. On the first three Wednesdays in May, children were dipped three times against the sun and dragged three times around the well in the same direction.

ST.LEVANS [3811 2198]. This well is located above Porthchapel beach, overlooking the cliffs. It now consists of an open structure with the water at ground level, supposedly good for eye conditions and toothache. Chapel of St.Selevan was nearby on cliffs.

LOWER BOSCASWELL [3765 3470]. At the end of Boscaswell Village, near Geevor mine behind a row of houses. Well consists of a rectangular enclosure with steps leading down to the water. Famed for leeches used in healing. Chapel once stood nearby.

TREGAMINION [4015 3587]. The site of this well is in a dramatic position, in a paddock of land beside the coastal path near Morvah. It was considered destroyed when a pump station was built there, but was then 're-discovered' in the 1990s, though the supposed 'well' may in fact only be a drain.

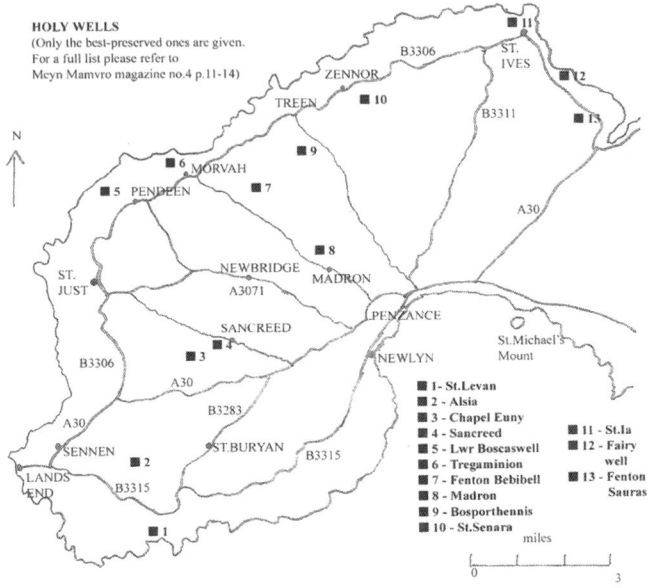

HOLY WELLS
(Only the best-preserved ones are given.
For a full list please refer to
Meyn Mamvro magazine no.4 p.11-14)

1 - St.Levan
2 - Alsia
3 - Chapel Euny
4 - Sancreed
5 - Lwr Boscaswell
6 - Tregaminion
7 - Fenton Bebibell
8 - Madron
9 - Bosporthennis
10 - St.Senara
11 - St.Ia
12 - Fairy well
13 - Fenton Sauras

FENTON BEBIBELL [4296 3520]. Near Four Parishes stone at end of lane past the Mên-an-Tol. This well, which consists of a chamber in the ground with a running stream, is translated as "Well of the Little People" perhaps referring to the fairy folk, or to the custom of little girls taking up their dolls to be blessed in the well on Good Fridays. Recently, this custom has been revived, and every year on Good Friday a small Group go to keep the well clear.

BOSPORTHENNIS [4395 3633]. This healing well lies in marshy ground hidden among reeds beside a small stream running through Bosporthennis Farm. The stone surround to the well is still in place and the water flows from a spring. It was once known to be as good as Madron Well, and children were taken to be cured of skin diseases in the same way.

ST.SENARA [4595 3822]. St.Senara is the matron saint of Zennor Church (and is probably based on Azenora, a pagan Celtic princess). Her well, which has recently been rediscovered, lies in a thicket beside a path leading off the B3306 road to Foage Farm. It consists of a massive block of granite on small stones over a spring flowing into a pool.

ST.IA [4147 4073]. Restored well-house just above Porthmeor beach in St.Ives. St.Ia arrived in Cornwall in the 5thC on a leaf, making her a probable vegetation Goddess.

FAIRY WELL [5337 3880]. Also known as St.Uny's well, this well is reached by a track leading off the coastal path at Carbis Bay through a beautiful nut grove. A steep descent leads to an enchanting well that issues from a low rock fissure and tumbles down to the beach below. Famed as a wishing well, providing that the wishes are spoken silently.

FENTON SAURAS [5423 3690]. This well lies in the grounds of the old Abbey at Tredreath at Lelant, near St.Ives, now converted into a private house (behind Well Cottage). Recently uncovered and cleared. An unusual two storey well in pretty setting.
Full details of these and other wells may be found in the book 'Fentynyow Kernow' and in a 2 part article 'The Forgotten Wells of West Penwith' in Meyn Mamvro nos. 51 & 52.